Reflections from the Heart

Zainool Hamid

Contents

1. Where Are You, My Dearest?

Where are you, my dearest?

I am like a child without its mother.

I am lost without your presence,

Like a man without his lover.

Time is moving so slowly,

Like a river up a hill.

I think of you constantly,

Like I never knew I will.

Come back to me quickly.

Please do not delay.

And make all things complete.

And make it stay that way.

I never knew you were my soul mate.

I knew you were my friend.

I should've known a long time ago,

We'd be together again.

My heart is sad; there are tears in my eyes.

All I do is whine.

I miss your warm and tender body

Cuddling next to mine.

2. Hold Out Your Hands to Me

Hold out your hands to me,

let me touch you with a smile.

Let me love you forever.

Not only for a little while.

Take away all I have without regrets.

All I possess I will gladly give.

You are all I ever wanted,

as long as I may live.

My life is now complete,

with our love we share.

I can think of nothing else

left in this world to care.

You are an angel sent to me.

From the one above.

I will always cherish you

and give you all my love.

+ + +

3. There Is No Time to Waste

There is no time to waste.

There is nothing standing in our way.

Are you brave enough to take this step,

Or are you happy as it stays?

Change can sometimes be difficult,

after years being set in your ways.

But this is a once-in-a-lifetime chance

to grab a little happiness that stays.

Do not be reluctant.

Do not hesitate.

I will be at your side as an anchor,

to steady the ship in case.

+ + +

4. Each Day Is Special

Each day is special.

Every day a gift.

Live life to the fullest,

you will not miss.

Stop and smell the roses

as you go on your way.

Send kisses and praises to all

as you say your prayers each day.

Who knows what tomorrow brings,

as life is so uncertain?

Tomorrow might be too late

as we face the final curtain.

Take all you can with both hands,

and be happy as you do.

This Ferris wheel comes around only once

and never comes back through.

+ + +

5. Tomorrow Is Too Far Away

Tomorrow is too far away,

like a tunnel without an end,

like waiting forever

just to see a friend.

Hours and days stand still,

as if frozen awhile.

Away from you seems longer

and longer each time.

Soon my arms will get to hold you,

and time again will do it.

My heart will be beating fast,

and faster by the minute.

+ + +

6. My Thoughts Are of You, Dear

My thoughts are of you, dear,

just wishing you were here.

Thinking of the times we had.

Now I am lonely and sad.

Tomorrow will be another day.

A day just like today.

I will still be missing you,

like I always do.

Lost and wandering around,

like a scentless hound.

I look left then right,

no Myah in my sight.

Crying while waiting is what I will do.

Counting the days till I see you.

It appears to be too long a wait,

to be with you and have another date.

+ + +

7. It Is a Special Artform

It is a special artform

to see a show come to life.

So many talents

to make it just right.

The stage is dark,

the performers are ready,

the spotlights are lit,

the audience is uneasy.

The curtains are drawn,

the mood is all set.

The performance starts

to a rousing success.

Bows are now taken.

Ovations are very loud.

All this coming together

is reflected by the crowd.

It is time to mingle

and listen to the critics.

Take opinions from every one

and pretend that you like it.

+ + +

8. When You Think You Are Secure

When you think you are secure

and everything is sound.

You meet the same people

on the way up and down

Pick your friends carefully.

Make judgments as you need to.

Make your decisions on the facts,

not emotions or untruth.

A kind word spoken is like music,

it soothes and calms the mind.

It gives a lot of satisfaction,

and an encouraging sign.

Make decisions you can live with,

nothing in this lifetime is set in stone.

Changes are continuously changing,

To all known and unknown.

Your choice will be the right one,

made from careful study.

All that is yours

will be yours only.

+ + +

9. As the Rays of the Sun

As the rays of the sun

change the leaves on the trees in the distance to a differ-

ent mood,

as the evening melts away into night,

I think of you.

As the sunlight still lingers

making the day a golden hue.

and a reflection of your face on the water,

I think of you.

As the sun fades into darkness,

I remember the joy in your laughter,

and the happiness in your heart too.

I think of you.

As the night covers the day with its darkness,

and the stars pop out to see,

and the moon stands in cue,

I THINK OF YOU.

+ + +

10. Like a Speck in This Gigantic World

Like a speck in this gigantic world,

insignificant and unimportant,

looks around for some enlightenment

but lies dormant,

intolerance leaves no room for improvement.

Encouragement is priceless,

working to achieve a goal

while untangling the tangled mess.

Make your mark wherever you may.

Leave an impression, if only in your mind.

Let all your belief and philosophy

lift you in your climb.

Nothing is achieved without effort,

and what is accomplished is creation.

Take pride and joy in your talent,

and all you touch will blossom.

+ + +

11. These Words I Write Can Tell a Story

These words I write can tell a story.

They originated deep in my heart.

I'll try to explain all that expired

And begin at the start.

You knew I was your first love.

I somehow knew that too.

My hope was someday

To get back together with you.

You went your way and I went mine,

A few times we crossed paths.

You never knew, but I knew

You've always had my heart.

Seeing you at that window

Is imprinted in my mind.

You belonged to another then,

And I was left behind

A love made in heaven

Has returned to me.

All of life's experiences

Made it clear for us to see

Have no doubt about it:

It was not an easy journey.

Some days were very hard,

And nothing was easy.

A road traveled once before

Has many hidden secrets.

But when you know your way around,

You learn to hide the weakness.

One pure in heart right from the start

Can tell its true meaning.

Nothing is lost at no great cost.

We can still capture that feeling.

When we were young,

Time was not a factor.

But as we got older,

It really does matter.

+ + +

12. How Can I Explain This Feeling?

How can I explain this feeling

when I am with you?

That feeling of being with someone,

with a love you always knew.

That someone you have reunited with,

way back in your past,

that stole your heart again

and promised love would last.

A chance for that love

to blossom once again.

It stood the test of time

and welcomed all the change.

Now I can see the future

with you at my side.

I would want for nothing else

but to have our love survive.

+ + +

13. How Does It Feel When We Hold Hands?

How does it feel when we hold hands?

How do you feel when we touch?

Is it magical and electric,

or is it a rush?

What do you see when you look into my eyes?

Is it bright and inviting?

Is it what you expected,

or is it exciting?

Is the spark gone on once again,

like a lamp in the night?

Is a warm wind blowing,

scattering love and kisses alike?

Are your doubts real or imagined?

Only you know the answer.

Sometimes a thought

is heard in a whisper.

+ + +

14. View Your Preference Behind a Curtain

View your preference behind a curtain.

Let no one see your fear.

Look carefully while making judgment,

trying not to be unfair.

Hidden and not revealing anything,

sooner or later it becomes transparent.

Looking through a distorted vision,

nothing is apparent.

What is seen is hard to believe,

even harder to conceive.

The reality of life transformed

is so alive and real.

Wake up and acknowledge life,

so precious and so surreal.

Take flight from all the restrictions,

and trust in what you feel.

+ + +

15. Today Will Produce Many Wonders

Today will produce many wonders.

How many—who knows?

Like the sun the wind, the moon and sea,

and a complex rose.

A new baby is given life.

A flower blooms in the desert.

Water flows into the valley,

and the rain makes everything wet.

Smiles are seen all around.

Children are at play outside.

Animals are roaming all about

in the savannahs so wide.

Lovers will be holding hands

while walking along the seashore.

Moonlight will be beaming down,

and so much more.

A few miracles are given,

like sight to the blind,

hope to the desperate,

and what we lost we will find.

+ + +

16. How Much Do I Love You?

How much do I love you?

How do you remove fear?

How much do I miss you?

How do you measure care?

I take nothing for granted.

Not even your love for me.

In life there are so many changes.

That is the reality.

A pillar of strength sets a foundation

to blossom and to grow.

Your trust and understanding

is all I need to know.

Your love to me is precious

and sacred as life itself.

Just sharing your love with me—

I can ask for nothing else.

+ + +

17. How Can I Judge and Not Be Judged?

How can I judge and not be judged?

How do I see injustice

and look the other way?

How do I correct the negative

when no one prays?

When hope is gone and all appears lost,

an appeal to your God

is all there left to do.

Let yourself feel the power

from whatever you think is true.

Truth has a way of finding the light,

however long you keep it in the dark.

Remember there can be many fires

lit from a single spark.

All is not lost. Human kindness still exists,

and love is what it will send.

Together we can correct all the injustice

that was left to mend.

+ + +

18. Words Cut Deeper Than a Knife

Words cut deeper than a knife

when spoken in hate.

But a kiss cannot heal that wound

with a simple peck on the face.

How do you chose what others say

if they say words of love in hate?

Listen and learn from experience

and leave it all to faith.

The demon haunts my mind

like a shadow that always lingers.

I battle all these emotions

like a student and a teacher.

I cannot change a single thing

however hard I try.

A moment seen that sheds a light

on something that has died:

observe from a distant

without a comment,

like a fly on the wall,

I am noticeably silent.

+ + +

19. Mobile Mirror

Reality is like a mirror

looking back at you.

Hide your face and feelings;

it will see through you.

What you think you can hide

and who you try to deceive

will show bight and clear

to untangle the mess you weave.

Reflections are not all you see.

Look deeper into your own eyes.

What you see is reality.

Truth is never a surprise.

Paint a picture to cover up the image.

However hard you try,

nothing can be washed away

by the tears that you cry.

+ + +

20. Memories Are Like Magnets

Memories are like magnets;

They keep pulling you to the past.

But destiny and the future

Is a reminder of what will last.

Reflections of light on waterdrops

Look exactly like a diamond.

The future is so uncertain,

Like the rising of the morning sun.

Tomorrow is another day.

Today is all there is.

To look beyond is speculative.

Life is a pilgrimage.

Love is a feeling of total bliss

And can only be felt

When all is aligned in your mind.

It will make your heart melt.

21. The Little Sign You See Each Day

The little sign you see each day

Will make you go or make you stay

Hugs and kisses go away

Your feelings are in disarray

No plans no demands

Is the norm after the storm

The light at the end of the tunnel

Is dimming and losing its form

Most road traveled

Reaching toward that goal

Endlessly searching for love

But ending up alone

Hold on to what you are

Never sway

You are the master

You are the final say

+ + +

22. If You Have Nothing

If you have nothing

You want for nothing

If you want nothing

You already have everything

Possession is only of self

And can be nothing else

Like a breeze passing by

That sooner or later dies

Time is all that's left for the living

While counting all the pieces

Like howling at the moon

And laughing at the masses

Your thoughts are your own

That generate your true feelings

Hidden in strange places

And are ever so revealing

+ + +

23. A Mystery Is What You Are

A mystery is what you are:

A guiding light and rock.

A sturdy ship in a storm,

Guided by your luck and touch.

Invisible in other eyes

But seen in plain view.

A light shining so very bright.

You are always you.

My world is so much better

Now that you are in my life.

Your beauty starts the sparks

That allows me to strive.

There are no regrets,

Only thanks and praise.

All I have been given, so thankful,

I accept in so many ways.

Those things we did together

Will always live in my mind.

A memory to build upon

With someone like you so fine.

My heart is yours forever.

My love will grow every day.

I live to make you happy,

Each and every way.

+ + +

24. My Heart Is Yours Forever

My heart is yours forever.

My love for you grows every day.

I will live to make you happy

in every possible way.

You are like a fresh wind

blowing in from the past.

And stirring up excitement,

the feelings of my heart.

My life has new meaning

by the way you make me feel.

When I am near you,

all things appear so real.

Nothing shall come between us.

Love will be our mantra.

We will live for each other,

for now, and forever.

+ + +

25. Facts and Truth Are Different

Facts and truth are different,

even though they complement.

When love and life are in harmony.

Happiness has no end.

Truth is a feeling deep down

that controls your every action.

Fact is just knowing,

creating a reaction.

Some things appear like others,

like a shadow in the wind.

The night becomes the morning,

and the rivers are fed by springs.

What is real or un-real—

is it magical or mystical?

Is what the eyes see

the truth or what's factual?

+ + +

26. The Future of Awesome

The future of awesome

The brightness of dark

The belief of doubt

The knowledge of smart

The height of loneliness

The depth of nothingness

The sight of thought

The abundance of emptiness

The ultimate of style

The stagnation of fashion

The undermining of thought

The prediction of passion

The color of trust

The weight of worth

The motion of stillness

The graduation of girth

The beauty of ugly

The emotion of calm

The brilliance of dark

The infection of charm

The magic of mystery

The sound of silence

The end of the beginning

The splendor of simplicity

The denial of ego

The secrets that don't exist

The disguise without a mask

The simple is the easy fix

The ballad of odors

The union of divorce

The vex of understanding

The found and the lost

+ + +

27. Fear Not My Little One

Fear not my little one,

the fruit of life is abundant.

Feast upon the love that's shared.

Do not be despondent.

The time is now to get your fill.

It will soon be gone like a storm,

like the blooming daffodils,

looking prettiest at the break of dawn.

Take all you can. There is no charge.

Like a dream, this too shall pass.

A new change will take its place,

just another splendor in the grass—

like the changing hues of the sunsets,

like the honeybee and its golden nectar,

like the mountain reaching for the sky,

like all things wholesome as you are.

+ + +

28. Teach Me to Love You Better

Teach me to love you better.

My only joy is to please you.

My wish is that you are always glad,

And I never ever make you sad.

Show me where I should touch you.

Show me the things that please you.

I want to learn all I can in haste,

Just to put that smile on your face.

I have been wrong before, you know,

But never about you.

To make this love of ours grow,

Teach me all I need to know.

Your touch is like magic

Your personality I adore.

You are all I ever needed,

I cannot want for more.

+ + +

29. Another Day without You

Another day without you,

and the day has just begun.

A lonely empty feeling,

like remembering a sad song.

This space that separates us now

was never meant to be.

We were meant to be together,

for all the world to see.

I count each day without you,

and wish with all my heart,

we will soon get together,

and never ever part.

My love for you has grown

at a very rapid pace,

written on my face.

+ + +

30. How Do You Become a Perfect Human Being?

How do you become a perfect human being,

or is it a fanciful dream?

Good thoughts and deeds

only touch the surface, it seems.

First self is the main focus,

to maintain health and calm,

and see this world for what it is,

a paradise and a sham.

Dreams and hope are promises,

if only in your mind.

They only come to life

when all the stars align.

The endless possibilities

that life will reveal

can only be experienced

when everything is real.

Shadows disappear with light,

the same light that created the shadow.

All is not what it appears to be,

sometimes vain and shallow.

+ + +

31. If I Had the World, I Would Give It to You

If I had the world, I would give it to you.

But all I have is love to give you.

My admiration and respect for you

Are greater than I ever knew.

I LOVE YOU, MYAH.

u r d fire

A love affair that's meant to be

Lay dormant but not dead.

It has once again blossomed

To a love story instead.

As we live in this world each day,

Who knows how life unfolds?

To have your love come back to me

Is something to behold.

God has once again

Fulfilled a dream for me

By making our two hearts come together,

As it was always meant to be.

You are the fire.

Myah Myah.

+ + +

32. Thinking of You, I Am Lost in a Dream

Thinking of you, I am lost in a dream.

The image of your face is imprinted.

All things that I see around me

Remind me of you instead.

Words are easy to say

When you are romancing.

When the facts are known,

Only then all is knowing.

Negativity is easy to create;

It is the same as hate,

Created by bad thoughts and deeds

And the lack of faith.

Help me to see the fortunes

And all I now possess,

And rid my thoughts and mind

Of all that uselessness.

+ + +

33. You Let Your Scent Linger

You let your scent linger,

like an intoxicating mist.

I reach out to hold you

and touch your face with a kiss.

True love is the joy of life.

Eddies are never motionless.

Impetus corrects its own mistakes.

Truth would surface nevertheless.

Emotions often trigger memories

while desires and lust are fighting.

Satisfaction only last a while,

but life is left smiling.

The sun's rays focus on your face,

and your smile lights up the morning.

Joy is in the air and all around.

My love is overflowing.

Action is spurred on by want.

Truth is surround by doubt.

The uttered word is your bond

in a whisper or a shout.

+ + +

34. You Are My New Inspiration

You are my new inspiration.

Enabling me to write these words.

They flow out of me like a faucet.

Where they come from, who knows?

Your face and smile light up the room.

You stand out like a blossoming rose.

Your beauty is unmatchable.

I am not the only one who knows.

A light that shines from your eyes

sets a spark throughout the room.

Your presence flutters my heart,

and nothing else is of concern.

A feeling I can't describe,

however hard I try.

Whenever I am with you,

love materializes.

+ + +

35. You Are Perfect Like a Flower That Has Blossomed from a Bud

You are perfect like a flower that has blossomed from

a bud,

pouring from its chalice of beauty all your sweetness

and hugs.

An image in my mind

paints a picture of you.

A smile comes to my face,

and my love is renewed.

Like an angel sent to love me.

Like a dream that I have so often.

I live in the splendor of you,

moment by moment.

Clouds drifting across the sky

remind me of you.

Your smile lights up my life

and displays all your beauty.

In search of wealth,

we give up so much to get so few.

In search of your love,

there was nothing I wouldn't do.

36. Tender Words Spoken from the Heart

Tender words spoken from the heart

And not your lips

That fluttering butterfly feeling felt when greeted with

a kiss

Holding you strengthens my soul

Touching you is like a fireball exploding

I place your hand in mine

All the sounds and light are awakened

As the sun's rays filter through the clouds

As the wind pushes it to and fro

I see beauty in your eyes

And so much more

+ + +

37. Love Does Not Know Its Depth till Separation

Love does not know its depth till separation.

Love is joy and sorrow.

Love is oh! so understanding.

Love will be here tomorrow.

The scent of you that fills the air

is absent when you are gone.

I reach out to touch you

each day at the break of dawn.

Tomorrow is far away.

Hopeful dreams fulfill,

like the far-off mountain top

that started as a hill.

Your touch would be like a fire

when next we meet again.

The first touch would burn my fingers

but I will feel no pain.

You are the reason for life again,

this longing in my heart,

those precious times we had together.

I dread each day we are apart.

Thoughts of you get into my head

each time I am away from you.

I can't wait to touch you again

and share my love too.

+ + +

38. I Have This Feeling Deep Inside Me

I have this feeling deep inside me.

I don't know what it is.

All I know I can't live without you.

Hopefully I never will.

I dream of you at night often.

My thoughts are only of you.

My days are long without you.

It's your love that sees me through.

Take away those thoughts of mine,

that love cannot last forever.

This feeling of love is not only now.

It's forever and ever.

I have this feeling deep inside me.

I do know what it is.

I know I cannot live without your love.

Hopefully I never will.

+ + +

39. As the Sun Moves Over for the Moon

As the sun moves over for the moon,

and the skies turn purple gray—

as the darkness covers the scene,

and roosting birds find their way—

like mountains in the distance

that appear painted in blue—

the brilliant sunlight dimming,

so my thoughts go back to you.

I watch in silent wonder

as the day turns into night.

I see the hues changing

as darkness replaces the light.

It is no wonder I feel the way I do,

just knowing that you are there.

I look forward to every day

in this new life we share.

+ + +

40. At Peace with Your Inner Self

At peace with your inner self

And thoughts of a peaceful existence

Let the mind control all

And make all decisions

A smile is a sign of satisfaction

A smile we can control

Time and death we cannot change

Just like getting old

We can change so many things

As many as we can handle

But things we cannot change

We try so hard to dismantle

To be in a peaceful world

We must learn to forgive

In time we will forget

And the burden will be lifted

Touch the spirit of the moment

Take time to taste the vibe

Delay not for any reason

For what is left is precious and alive

+ + +

41. Do Not Wonder If the Day Is Over

Do not wonder if the day is over.

The sun will set, the moon will appear.

The shadows will cast a long trail.

The skies will turn gray.

And the moon will glow

to show the way.

The sun has exploded the colors

as the sky changes its golden glow.

The sunset in the distance,

a prelude to a greater show.

The golden light fades into darkness

as slowly as a mountain crab.

And the evening slowly drifts away

into the darkness of the dark.

The moon drifts from behind the clouds

and fills the valley with love.

All is lit with expectation

beaming from above.

Tomorrow a new cycle will form

to repeat the beauty of yesterday.

All the elements are put in place.

The sun will lead the way.

Fear not what time has taken away,

for wisdom is gained from time.

Nothing is lost—enormous gains—

with the eventual passing of time.

42. As I Watch the Tiny Finches Fly in Their Zig-Zag Fashion

As I watch the tiny finches fly in their zig-zag fashion

Around the bright color of the ripening fruit tree

I watch the bluebirds coming and going

So carefree and fancy free

As the sun rises above the landscape

As the fluffy cloud formations drift

I see your face and all your form

In a perfect frame it fits

Memories of our distant past

Come flooding back sometimes

Like when we held hands and kissed

And had to say goodbye

+ + +

43. As the Darkness Covers the Day

As the darkness covers the day

And the angles all assemble for prayer,

As the sunlight disappears,

It's time to reflect.

Things you could have shown.

Things you could have said

Or done instead,

Never realizing what it meant.

Looking beyond the darkness,

The light reveals a real reflection,

Like a mirror in the ocean.

What is seen is a true image.

As the sparkle of raindrops in the sunlight,

As the mountains peaks reaching for the sky,

As I watch the angels learning how to fly,

I sit and wonder why.

What did time give us,

If only to a limit?

To time we must commit.

To time we must submit.

+ + +

44. Can I Love You More, Can I Miss You More?

Can I love you more, can I miss you more?

I am here and you are there

on another shore.

My heart reaches out, my voice is loud.

I want to touch you

and show you my love.

Days are long and nights are long

When I am away from you, dear.

Time races by when we are together,

whether we are here or there or wherever.

Is there a timeline set in stone,

never to be tampered with?

Do we live our lives in a designed path,

without a way to change it?

Space and time are against us.

But this too shall pass,

like your head on my pillow,

or the sand in the hourglass.

Fear not for what lies ahead,

for we cannot see the future.

But counting all our blessings,

we surely came out the winner.

Embrace the moment joyfully.

Let every moment last.

Together we can get the rewards

from a love born in the past.

Like birds soaring in the wind,

we will fly to explore new shores.

And we will paint our own picture

of the beauty that we saw.

45. Wish I Could Bring Back the Past and Share It with You

Wish I could bring back the past and share it with you

But that can never be

Loving you, every day left is a gift that I will cherish

endlessly

Lives going in different directions

Sometimes they never meet

But not so in our instant

We were destined to greet

Thoughts of what would have happened

As life so mysteriously unfolds

If what was meant to be will be

Or is it the fulfilment of a dream?

46. Life Is So Unpredictable

Life is so unpredictable,

full of joys and sorrows.

Live life fully today,

and do the same tomorrow.

The day has many wonders

everywhere you look.

Some we see so clearly,

some are pictures in a book.

Take nothing for granted.

The world is at your feet.

Give respect and share your love

with everyone you meet.

Touch everyone you greet

in a very special way.

Wish them all good fortune

and happiness in their day.

The sun will disappear in the west

as the day turns into night.

The mystery of life is told

to all who see the light.

GOD BLESS YOU, MYAH.

47. What Do You Say . . . Let's Go to Parlatuvier Today

What do you say . . . let's go to Parlatuvier today.

We will sit at the hilltop overlooking the bay.

The fishing boats anchored to ropes, tied to the shore.

The waves will be breaking softly on the ocean's surface.

We will explore the hillsides and marvel at this sight.

We will put our feet in the water, and dance away the

night.

A view with such beauty, a peaceful sight to sea.

A heaven here on earth, just made for you and me.

All that surrounds us, we will remember with great joy.

A beauty we will add to but never ever destroy.

The blue waters protected by this cove instead,

Like loving arms wrapped around a baby's head.

+ + +

48. I See the Crystal Waters Falling Off Your Face

I see the crystal waters falling off your face

I see your true beauty and your grace

I see the sunset paint its colors on your hair

As the butterflies and hummingbirds hurry off in pairs

I see the beauty by the pleasure in your smile

I see your love for the outdoors and the wild

I see your strength in many things as your eyes light up in

Williamsville

Old friends are dear to you in many ways

The joy you have from old stories and tales

The loyalty I admire is true in you

In everything you say and do

The true joy is felt within

Like the love of an offspring

You carry with you such confidence

Always thinking in advance

49. In a Flash

In a flash,

a memory is formed.

Remembered forever,

like a bad storm.

Mankind is evolving.

So many uncertainties.

Like the wind,

changing constantly.

Wise men always said,

Take things as they appear.

Never try to change it.

All will soon be clear.

Walking tall and proud,

Head held high,

no known format

for who lives or dies.

How do you account for the beauty around you?

How do you praise the sun and moon?

How do you explain that feeling

when you hear your favorite tune?

+ + +

50. I See the Sun Peeping through the Trees

I see the sun peeping through the trees,

the mountain bathed in blue.

Sparrows fly in pairs to feed.

The day begins anew.

The air is crisp and invigorating

as we stand on the hillside,

as we look down into the valley

at the village scattered far and wide.

The mist has lifted above the canopy.

The air is pushed by the ocean breeze.

In the clearing we can see a village,

far away from the winter freeze.

As the sun heats up the morning,

the air is charged with wonder.

The day enfolds its beauty

from the great yonder.

The day is in full bloom

as the moments ticks away . . .

just making a memory

is all we take away.

+ + +

51. My Thoughts Are of You Consistently

My thoughts are of you consistently.

Is that love?

My happiest times are with you.

Is that love?

Your presence excites me.

Is this love?

You are everything I ever wanted.

Is that love?

Afraid to lose you.

Is that love?

Butterflies when we touch.

Is that love?

My highest respect is for you.

Is that love?

I see the kindness of your heart.

Is that love?

THAT'S THE WAY I FEEL.

IT MUST BE LOVE.

+ + +

52. I Miss You and You Miss Me

I miss you and you miss me.

Together we sing the same poetry.

What can be done to fix this,

or is it meant to be like this?

I miss you and you miss me.

That is the reality.

What we do about it

is still a mystery.

Sad eyes and tears are shed,

lonely days and nights instead.

What to do?

I am away from you.

A lonely cry in the night

when no one is in sight.

A feeling of desperation

from this separation.

A hurting cry in the wilderness

about someone I miss.

Another night and day,

and you are still so far away.

+ + +

53. Truth Is Trust

Truth is trust.

It's up to us.

Be true to you,

And all will renew.

Like a spark's short life,

the truth soon comes to light.

Nothing stays hidden long,

if at first it was wrong.

To thy self be true.

Nothing new.

True to a commitment,

right until the end.

The reflection in the mirror

is not of another.

What is seen is no other

than you and your honor.

A love in your heart,

the truth from the start.

A fleeing of satisfaction.

A life in blissful union.

+ + +

54. Space and Time Are Not My Friend Today

Space and time are not my friend today,

when I think of you so far away.

I reach out to touch your hand.

The reality I understand.

The hurt cut deep inside my heart

the longer we are apart.

I think of the time we'll meet again,

and this hurt will have an end.

Until then, I must confess,

I cannot love you any less.

My love grows with every passing moment,

forever alive, never dormant.

Keep a smile upon your face.

Never a moment we must waste.

What is left no one knows.

Not your friends nor your foes.

55. I Want to Have a Talk with God

I want to have a talk with God.

But how do you do that?

I always wanted to,

since I was a little brat.

First I will say praises.

Then I will say thanks

for all that was given me

to make my life enhanced.

I want to thank God for the mountain,

the sun, the sea, and the sky.

Thanks for the rain and wind,

and all animals and birds that fly.

I want to pledge my devotion

to him and him alone,

and always have a prayer at hand,

to sing and chant or croon.

There will be so much I want to ask,

like death and love and happiness,

like neighbors, friends, and togetherness,

and can everything wrong be fixed.

I will ask God for a rule book

and a guide for the world to see,

and beg him to forgive everyone

and set the whole world free.

I will ask for sickness to be eradicated

and forgiveness to all,

no matter how big it is

or how very small.

I want to thank God for you

and the precious person you are,

Myah Myah.

56. Accept What Is

Accept what is.

Let go of what was.

Have faith in what will be.

And you will be free.

Love with all your heart.

Trust in what you do.

Keep a smile on your face.

Happiness will find you.

Reality has a way of setting the course

And makes the rules we play.

All your dreams you can put away

Or save it for a rainy day.

A new life has begun.

A new song will be sung.

The time has finally come

To love with all, not only some.

Pick up your fences.

Open up your heart.

Build more bridges.

Love will create a path.

+ + +

57. Reality Is an Activity in Consciousness

Reality is an activity in consciousness,

And so is the choice to be free.

Like the realms of the unknown,

Lost in a state of uncertainty,

It is not written like lines in a book—

The rules that apply to all who look.

Like the wind and the elements,

All will end, just as it was meant.

Trying to change

Or rearrange the game

With its ever-changing rules,

Only the goal remains the same.

Before your eyes, it's there to see.

What was meant to be, will be.

But consciously and subconsciously we see

The ever-changing reality.

Now is the reality that exists.

It can change in a blink.

Take advantage of every moment.

It can be over in a wink.

Let's be thankful for what we shared,

The beauty we have seen.

These memories we must cherish forever,

And everything in between.

Hold my hand and lean on me.

Together we'll face what will be.

I will be your everything,

And we'll adjust to reality.

58. My Days Are Full of Loneliness

My days are full of loneliness

and thoughts of you all day.

I occupy them with happy thoughts of you

and watch them fade away.

I see your image in everything

from a flower to a tree.

I see your face in my mind

with all its ecstasy.

Your eyes forever sparkle,

and your smile radiates

a kind of happiness

I see in your lovely face.

If I am dreaming,

don't wake me up.

I want to live this dream of you

and never have it stop.

When I think of you this way,

my thought are full of wonder.

I see so many fine qualities

without a single blunder.

+ + +

59. Another Sunset Has Come and Gone

Another sunset has come and gone

Without your precious company.

I sit and wonder why,

and why this has to be.

Gold and pink clouds cover the sky

like a blanket of protection.

Sunlight peeping through the mountains—

a moment of perfection.

All the colors of the sky

paint a picture in perfect unity.

The shadows and reflections

display all its hidden beauty.

I sit here in the dim light of dusk

while contemplating the day.

All colors seem to disappear

as the darkness has its way.

+ + +

60. Like the Wind That Gathers on the Hilltop

As the wind gathers on the hilltop

and gently kisses the treetops

as it flows to the valley below,

I watch in wonder.

As the clouds drift across the sky,

and form images of grandeur,

with colors so spectacular,

I watch in wonder.

As the waves of the ocean

break violently on the shore

with a sound of thunder,

I watch in wonder.

As I watch the rain fall

as it slowly turns to snow

and the rivers overflow,

I watch in wonder.

As I watch the children in masses,

attending to their classes,

as I see the future growing,

I watch in wonder.

Sunset and sunrise set the day

before the darkness takes over;

as the nighttime takes its place,

I watch in wonder.

My love for you has blossomed

by your beauty and your splendor,

so thankful you became my lover.

I am still in wonder.

61. How Do I Communicate My Love for You?

How do I communicate my love for you?

With smiles on my face and warmth in my heart.

I would want to pledge this love of mine,

And that would be my start.

Should I show my love with gifts

Scattered at your feet?

Or cover you with kisses

Every time we meet?

Should I praise your name

And shout it out loud on the mountaintop?

Or should I be humble

And suck it up?

Should I tremble at your touch

Or be nervous as a schoolboy

Who can't wait for your kiss

To give him greater joy?

How do you express your happiness

When the world is so right?

You share your fortune with others

And climb to higher heights.

To show your true feeling,

It must come from within:

An expression of love.

Pure happiness when you win.

+ + +

62. If You Can See the Shadows of My Pain

If you can see the shadows of my pain,

covered teardrops on the footprints of my life span,

it tells who I am.

If you see the warmth of my kindness,

and the joy of my existence, and for what I stand,

it tells you who I am.

If you walk in my shoes, and you know what I knew,

then you understand.

It tells who I am.

If you carry your pride and your smile like a crown, so

proud of your achievements,

always with an open mind,

it tells who I am.

If your beliefs, faith, and devotion, with all the dedication

to people you love, make you a man,

it's who I am.

I am not a stationary stone afraid of the unknown, a need

to experience all, big or small,

a devoted fan.

It tells who I am.

A simple man is who I am, and my consciousness always expands to full the voids of the now.

+ + +

63. What Was Shown to Us

What was shown to us

Was even more hideous,

Unlike what we know

Or what was ever shown before.

Serpents twisted in impossible positions.

Faces of pain in contorted conditions.

Life seems difficult to understand,

A supreme test to any man.

Molten rocks and hidden caves.

Displays of colors intermix like waves.

Breezes blowing to and fro,

With not a care for where it goes.

Light bouncing only from one end

While throwing shadows on white sand.

A force not easy to see

Pushes the imagination to the tenth degree.

Fear is an uncontrollable state

When there is nothing left but faith,

Like a feeling felt only then,

And back to reality again.

The aura that fills my space

Is overflowing with love and gratitude.

My emotions are abundant with joy and bubbling with a positive attitude.

+ + +

64. Muffled in Silence and Unseen Fright

Muffled in silence and unseen fright,

memories of the past flash like a light.

Remembering unknown elements,

a flashback to present tense.

All details remain hidden at times,

afraid to confess to their own demise.

A trumped-up opinion is revealed,

and that is when a promise is sealed.

Assembling all in one place, in haste,

and having encountered all, face to face,

what appeared so real before

was just a feeling, nothing more.

Many things are in focus now,

while others are in view.

Never try to conceal what's real

by creating something new.

The truth can only free your mind

if spoken from a heart that's kind.

Any secret truly revealed

can unlock that unbroken seal.

+ + +

65. Who Am I to Judge?

Who am I to judge?

Who am I to point my finger?

Why can't we look away

and tend to our own matters?

What you see is not the whole picture.

With many different points to view,

what is real and not seen

is sometimes hidden too.

Look with eyes that see beyond

accepting things with an open mind.

What is revealed is the truth.

In most things you will find

making assessments without the facts

can only lead to speculation.

Analysts and opinions

can only make accurate decisions.

With a frame of mind of distrust,

an option is soon formed.

Everything hidden from reality

Is soon revealed after the storm.

+ + +

66. Plant a Seed, Watch It Grow

Plant a seed, watch it grow.

How it turns out, no one knows.

Like hatchlings learning to fly—

a need to succeed with every try.

Some plants would flower

and produce sweet odors.

Some would grow into weeds

and are totally useless fodder.

To stand alone and fight the wind,

forever in a tailspin.

Not knowing the true art,

a pattern set by the past.

It's not easy to set a path.

But a try must come from the heart.

Nothing good comes from a lie.

No success without a try.

Lean on no one but in a God you trust;

the burden you create maybe unjust.

You will learn to live with it until you die,

and fight your battles as you cry.

+ + +

67. Sonnet

Shame and guilt cannot smile,

For they have no true feelings.

But love can blush, and kisses can touch,

With the effect and its true meaning.

Maybes and "I thought so" are not defined.

Like a sea of fishes, and no fishing line.

Like a shadow that soon goes away,

Leaving you helpless, empty and frayed.

Imagine a life without direction or goals,

Lost in the wilderness of lost souls.

Nothing to lose, nothing to gain.

Things changing but remaining the same.

The distance that keeps us apart

Is like an enemy to my heart.

+ + +

68. As Quiet as a Snowflake Falling

As quiet as a snowflake falling.

As colorful as a rose in bloom.

As distant as the sound of salvation.

As hopeless as a belief in doom.

Hope is a strength to believe in tomorrow.

Hope can build foundations today.

Hope is the pillar we can lean on.

Hope will take your fears away.

Yesterday is fading faster than a dream.

It's never thinking of tomorrow.

One cannot build a future

With past sadness and sorrows.

Tomorrow is a dream hope will fulfill.

Like the wounded, nursed back to health.

Hope is all that's left when all is lost.

Why not trust in God instead?

A matador's intention is to tire the bull.

A greedy man never gets his full.

The future will change your life whenever.

Nothing stays the same forever.

Looking through a window dimmed by the dust.

I can see the illusion and all the stuff.

Clarity is not clear when the mind is closed.

Making believe is just fooling your soul.

Fools—there are many that want to believe

When shadowed by their own disbelief.

Having all you want, and wanting more.

Only explain the metaphor.

Possession is of self and only physical.

Some only depend on the metaphysical.

Like a rose that shares to all its fragrance.

Wanting nothing, just spreading its essence.

+ + +

69. Beauty Comes in Many Forms

Beauty comes in many forms—

in a bouquet of fragrant flowers,

in a smile from a beautiful sunset

as it kisses the earth in the evening hours.

The sun's golden rays dance on the ocean

as they light up the evening sky—

a beauty to behold uniquely common

as the sunlight slowly dies.

A yellowish golden hue covers the evening

as the sun disappears from view—

a moment where shadows give birth

and everything is renewed.

As the rays of gold reflects on your face,

I see your beauty and your grace.

Each sunset tells a different story.

But I see all your inner beauty.

+ + +

70. How Do You Make a Foundation?

How do you make a foundation

Without a plan and a level?

How do you make it strong

Without mortar or a shovel?

Strength latches onto strength.

It ensures a successful union.

Together all can be achieved—

A much stronger fusion.

Things we learnt from what we saw

Set the boundaries for some.

Others were like a shining star,

Not waiting for anyone.

Magical, though mysterious,

Things always happen for the best.

To reach the top of the mountain.

You must take the first step.

Peace is accomplished

Only from within.

All exterior distractions

Only strengthen the mighty will.

The pure of heart have no fear

Of anything going wrong.

Truth and love and peace of mind

Are always all around.

+ + +

71. Innocuous and Such Were All I Was Taught

Innocuous and such were all I was taught

With my mind closed to all around me

Like the wind free to roam

And a flight to New York City

The world was a place to explore

Like an ocean far and wide

All things marveled me

Simplicity in its style

Basement shacks and windowless rooms

A palace of its own

A place to lay your thoughts down

and call this hole your home

White tiles on the countertop

Bunk beds in a row

No curtains were needed

To hide the filth and snow

Time spent in this reclusive place

Was brief but so enlightening

Not a day would pass

Without something exciting

This world was new and full of hope

And I was just about to see

New knowledge and J.A.P around us

and the freedom to be free

Days were full of adventures

Nights were so mysterious

Every high was so revealing

A joy to all around us

Lonely but puzzled by my forced exile

I joined in with full gusto

An education was the best decision

With future plans to join the show

Several years had passed

The dye was cast

Lonely turned into curiosity

A overdue journey home at last

Looking at all the changes at home

Trying to fit into the past

Between all the talent and beauty

Lies the fabric of its heart

Fascinated with this journey

I tried to claim my space

And was told quite sternly

I was the wrong race

Returning to the Big Apple

My future was on track

I never backed down

I was always on the attract

New doors would open

New opportunities would arrive

It was like a fairy tale

Suddenly come alive

A service engineer is what I was

Traveling here and there and everywhere

Putting out fires in your towns

Confident and with the fair with a flair

Traveling from the east to the west

A different challenge emerged

An introduction to television and movies

Was yet another test

The warmth of Los Angeles

Stimulates my mind

I looked for avenues

And many did I find

Love and marriage, children and responsibility

Set in motion a series of ventures

The hurt that's felt when one is dead

One must continue for the others

A new start was implemented

Independent and full of confidence

I returned to the workplace

With accolades from my friends

The loss of good friends

When you thought you had all you ever wanted

Life will have to start again

New challenges on the horizon

The journey has been stimulating

without a dull moment

I will do it all again and again

If I only can

+ + +

72. MYAH, My Love

There is a person who loves you,

who sees deeper than the surface.

Everything about you

puts a smile upon his face.

He admires the way you handle

the day-to-day chores.

Like an expert at work,

playing with your toys,

you are always so determined

to doing the right thing.

Your heart is in the right place.

Your praise I want to sing.

My love is still growing

by tremendous leaps and bounds.

I never want to see you cry,

or ever see you frown.

Today I send my love to you,

wherever you may be.

Together with kisses on a platter,

I'll send it off to thee.

+ + +

73. This House Is Lonely without You

This house is lonely without you.

Its emptiness saddens me.

I try to think of pleasant things,

but all I can see is empty.

Your shadows linger in the air,

like a sweet fragrance everywhere.

I often reach out to touch you,

but you're not there.

I count the days we are apart.

They appear to be longer.

I miss the morning and evening stroll.

Absence makes the heart fonder.

This too will pass, you always say,

like the rain and that lonely feeling.

But the hurt never goes away.

It accumulates like a bucket filling.

74. Fantasies Appear So Real

Fantasies appears so real.

They sometimes interchange.

What you thought you knew

and what you know

are frequently not the same.

Dancing pictures in my head

set in motion thoughts of you.

Dreams were all I had

to bring you into my view.

Dreams are free, not like reality.

Truth and time can support our trust.

What is real in our hearts,

and what is felt by both of us.

Fantasies can be misunderstood

if early in their formation.

The truth would reveal what's real,

eventually, with a solution.

Both are free, fantasies and reality.

We have little control of them personally.

How we use reality

to create a fantasy (or vice versa).

75. Like Fairy Tales

Like fairy tales

with happy endings—

a pleasant memory

of a happy harlequin.

Like massive rains and ferocious storms,

and a fearsome steady wind blowing.

Waves are tumbling into the darkness,

and the ships with their sails billowing—

a sight to behold

as the sun reflects on the water,

displaying magical colors,

like blue, green, and aqua.

The sunlight is golden brown

as it spreads its warmth in an embrace,

making everything so beautiful

in each and every place.

+ + +

76. A Physical Fence, an Emotional Barrier

A physical fence, an emotional barrier.

Tracks that devise ways to decide,

how to divide, the compromise.

Lies motionless but full of fire.

Looking across the lake at the mountaintop

the water seems forever as it stretches on.

The landscape appears to float in space,

and take on many figures and forms.

Endless is the way to salvation.

The devotion requires many commitments

Acknowledge the rewards and achievements,

and live with the satisfaction and accomplishments.

Can I feel love and see if it fits,

like a glove on a freezing morn?

Or paint my heart a golden glow

and avoid the wrath of the storm?

My mind goes wondering aimlessly,

thinking of nothing special or specific.

Just thoughts of days gone by,

some things nice and some things horrific.

Returning from the darkness,

coming into the light,

I am blinded by my ignorance

but not afraid to fight.

Each day in life is a journey.

What path you take is your own.

You can sink to the bottom of the pit

or be on top of the highest dome.

+ + +

77. Your Presence Reminds Me of Family

Your presence reminds me of family

The sharing and togetherness

Like returning to the past

And remembering the things we missed

Innocent and youth a powerful mix

With the future unknown

The venture to find our space

Would slowly unfold

Mixing of ideas

And sharing of dreams

Creating a new way

Full of extremes

Shadows disappear but memories don't

Like love in your heart that's true

So many things can change

But my love for you will never do

78. Everyone Has a Dream

Everyone has a dream.

Everyone wants a better tomorrow.

Everyone wants to be happy.

No one wants to experience sorrow.

A make-believe world we often make

to have a dream fulfilled.

Fake as it may be in reality,

to be real it never will.

Dreams are for dreamers,

like sun to a flower.

Your true love you hope

will be yours forever.

Take nothing for granted,

as life is so unpredictable.

Hold on to your dreams.

All things are attainable.

+ + +

79. Not Hearing from You Is Like a Drumbeat Beating Inside Me

Not hearing from you is like a drumbeat beating inside me,

wishing I had not left you behind

but stayed and faced the danger.

It has passed, this test of life,

like the many we have faced.

Many more would come our way.

We must not vacillate.

Memories are like eggs you store away,

for someday they would give birth.

Remembering things and learning from them

and gaining from all they're worth.

The heart is a mirror of your actions.

They stick together like glue.

They reveal so many things.

Everything about you.

80. This Morning I Awoke Loving You More

This morning I awoke loving you more,

wondering why I never felt this way before.

A night is not very long, they say.

But my love grew stronger in every way.

A sight of peace while you're asleep,

as you lay there amongst the sheets.

As the day morphed into dawn,

you lay there sleeping like one newly born.

I stood there amazed by what I was seeing,

thanking God for what I was given—

someone like you with all your beauty,

to love and cherish till eternity.

As you awake and the day comes to life,

your smile and your eyes shines a light.

Your presence is so fulfilling

to start the day with a beautiful morning.

+ + +

81. There Is No Time to Say Tomorrow

There is no time to say tomorrow.

No time to say it's the end.

There is no time to call it quits.

Never a time to quit on a friend.

No time to stay apart.

Take action from what's in your heart.

Gather all your happiness,

and rid yourself of loneliness.

Tomorrow is another day.

How many more, who can say?

A plan in place is a wise idea.

For your happiness and welfare is all I care.

Loneliness has many voices;

they sometimes say too much.

Like talking of a solution,

pretending there's no rush.

A blind man sees with his feel.

A hungry man's pain is real.

To a lonely man, time is wasted and such

on things that are not worth as much.

Time and tide waits for no one,

not even for a king.

In your fight with time,

time will always win.

+ + +

82. This Shadow That Follows Me Around

This shadow that follows me around,

not making a single sound.

Seeing things deep in my soul,

some secrets never to be told.

Tight lipped and on my shoulder,

and lighter than a feather.

My shadow sees all I do,

sometimes happy, sometimes blue.

Peeking over my shoulder,

sometimes getting bolder.

Casting images greater in size,

disappearing and appearing whenever it likes.

I have to befriend my shadow

and be a more mellow fellow.

Try to understand its plight

as it goes in and out of sight.

My shadow is attached to me,

like leaves on a banyan tree.

Like my shadow, you are always present,

in my every thought and moment.

+ + +

83. How Far We Have Traveled to Find the Love That Was So Close at Hand

How far we have traveled to find the love that was so close at hand.

Many roads traveled, and many years have passed.

We now understand.

What was true before would always be true.

However long it took, who knew

that you and I would find each other?

A mystery, we sometimes wonder.

In the shadows of the fading light,

I can see sunlight drifting off to night.

As the mountains disappear from sight,

I can see your face flickering in the light.

An image of you lingers in my mind.

The beauty you possess is so amazing.

A blessing from God was our reunion.

Finding each other again makes our life so fulfilling.

+ + +

84. Take Nothing for Granted

Take nothing for granted

Let no one take control

You alone can make your choices

You alone can control your world

Temptations are numerous

Distractions all around

Not all you encounter

Is always good and sound

Happiness and contentment

Are very hard to attain

Sometimes it is easy

It's always yourself to blame

A solid foundation on which to stand

An emotional state in balance

When harmony and rhythm are found

It's like a beautiful song and dance

Happiness can be found

Only on the inside

The outer beauty that we see

Is only there to disguise

All these thoughts fill my head

Whenever I think of you

I just wanted you to know

That my love for you is true

+ + +

85. When Love Comes Your Way, Grab It

When love comes your way, grab it

Before it goes away.

You may never find it again.

There might not be another day.

You have waited so long to find it.

Now it's here at last.

Wind your love around it.

Love with all your heart.

Things would have been different

If I'd never gone away.

But now that I found your love again,

I pray it's here to stay.

When love comes your way, grab it.

Never let it get away.

You may never find it again,

However hard you pray.

I am so glad I found you again.

My life has found a new meaning.

Together we can fulfill a dream.

That was there from the beginning.

+ + +

86. Be Humble, Not Proud

Be humble, not proud,

Alone or in a crowd,

Sight unseen.

What is apparent

Is concurrent.

It disappears and reappears,

Like a sunset.

Nothing missed.

Just a shift.

Add to the list.

Nothing amiss.

The color of emotions is pain.

The cycle that jewelry begins

In the family cycles of life origin.

Thrust in position to expedite future times,

Restrictions to you (or any other) as to the advancement,

internal to the structure.

Dragons are only in our minds.

So is depression.

Walk a mile in someone else's shoes and hope they fit.

A center line only stays centered if you don't move.

Friendships are like frogs; they are slippery and hard to hold.

As we create our own little world

And set up spikes around it,

Inviting all to enter,

Just to see who fits,

All that belongs to you is protected

With love and all the trimmings.

Strangers are always welcomed,

Only if they are winning.

Nothing matters but self.

Some people would say

They live only for themselves.

Not a care from day to day.

Spread your arms around your possessions.

Guard them with your wit.

They are not worth much.

Not even a little bit.

Others are important.

More important than you think.

Without your fellow humans,

Your life is sure to sink.

Mindful of others.

Respect for all around.

A rule to live by,

A belief good and sound.

Do not set up borders.

Let all around you in.

When love is in our heart,

Everyone wins.

Take time to smell the roses

As you travel through life's mysteries.

Gather all the beauty around you.

Make choices in life, not maybes.

God does not hide His face from anyone,

Just like the moon the wind and the sun.

Like the rain and stars above,

They are there for all to love.

The best things in life are free,

Just like life itself.

Be satisfied with what you have,

While gardening your wealth.

+ + +

87. In the Face of Greed One Must Let Go

In the face of greed one must let go.

What is given is of no consequence.

Give so others may prosper,

Only give freely; don't be hesitant.

Possessions are few and so precious.

They are only of self, nothing else.

Body, mind, and soul are all we possess;

They are all that is needed until death.

So give freely, for there is no cost.

No one wins who give the most.

Giving of self is the greatest gift.

Material possessions are only a myth.

Having the knowledge of mind control,

One can create emotions,

Together with a genuine soul,

And a vessel as a strong foundation.

A mind to make choices.

A soul to forgive.

A body to take the challenge.

All we can we should give.

+ + +

88. As the Sparrow Sings

As the sparrow sings

on the treetops up above.

I sit here

and wonder where you are,

my love.

It's been awhile since I saw you.

Time appears to have no end.

I count the days we are apart,

just hoping they will end.

The telephone rang, but no answer,

as thoughts go through my head.

Are you safe or in danger,

or are you thinking of me instead?

Tomorrow is a new beginning.

Another fairy tale has begun.

Many new and old feelings

will come together as one.

Where are you?

Where are you, my friend?

I count the days we're apart

Just hoping they will end.

89. In My Mind I Am Concerned

In my mind I am concerned,

confused and all alone.

I tried to forget and move on,

but hopelessly, I keep holding on.

When you left and said we were through,

I tried to understand.

My world just fell apart

and ended all our plans.

Raindrops on the rooftop

and the music that it makes.

take my mind off your leaving

as they transport me to a different state.

I must go on, as you must do,

to a happier place to be.

Somewhere true love is found

where it's happier for you and me.

Little is lost; so much is gained,

like knowing you have the wrong one,

and love can still be possible,

possible for everyone.

+ + +

90. It Is Not Too Late to Trust in Faith

It is not too late to trust in faith.

What is lost is naught.

What you thought was yours

Was not yours at all.

All you owe are thoughts.

Accumulating without gaining.

Hiding yet not concealing.

Giving with thoughts of receiving.

Smiling without feelings.

The other is your brother.

The world has many wonders.

Only you can give you,

In order to save the others.

Hello, and much more,

Lies beyond yonder land—

Awaits with faith

The mystery to understand.

Believing in something you don't understand.

Can lead to serious doubts.

Questions without answers,

Understanding the ins and outs.

91. You Always Speak the Truth

You always speak the truth

when you speak from the heart

Words are wind, they say

When spoken in haste

Look beyond the hopelessness

See with eyes of tomorrow

Always failure

Ends in sorrow

Love is free

And so are thoughts

Kindness and compassion

Are not taught

Only you can feel your pain

Only a honest man tells his gains

Only God can help the downtrodden

Making a place for them in heaven

92. It Is Not What You Achieved

It is not what you achieved,

but what you expect,

that makes you feel

you can win and be the best.

To look beyond,

you must first see the present.

The future is only shown

to those in heaven.

Make space for doubts.

There are no guarantees.

What you believe in,

only you can truly see.

Time is not enough

to know all you need to know.

It's your life choices

that make it so.

It's not only the tears that fall on my pillow

or the fog that hangs over the meadow

or the happiness and sorrow

that make me so mellow.

It is the world and its music,

and the love of all of it.

The life that we live

and the love that we give.

I sometimes sit and wonder,

there cannot be another

as beautiful as you, my lover.

I am blessed it is you and no other.

93. The Brief Glimpse of All Beauty

The brief glimpse of all beauty

does not reveal the depth of creation.

Beauty cannot be destroyed

when it is imbedded in emotions.

Thoughts and deeds are vessels

that cement the true emotions.

Bliss can only be achieved

by our own assorted actions.

A thought that shines but never flickers.

An anchor that hope can hold onto.

It's easiest for happiness to find someone already happy—

someone like you.

Today is where the future is.

Tomorrow will be.

Yesterday was a gift

given to all beings.

You were born with nothing.

You will leave with nothing.

All you should accumulate

are happiness and life's knowledge.

Thoughts and deeds

manage the mind.

Kindness and giving

are divine.

+ + +

94. How Do You Explain Loneliness?

How do you explain loneliness?

It is hidden, then appears like flashes

that jar the memories

like a storm in your mind,

tossing and overthinking its boundaries,

flashbacks to a different state.

And the mind wonders about

reality and negativity that poison the mind

and light the fire of doubt.

The wind kisses your face as it travels through to its

destination,

mixed with emotions and thoughts of past,

transporting you to some another illusion.

Faith and truth trust and love

are the foundation for a real relationship.

Respect and compromise

help to steady the ship.

+ + +

95. Away from You Is More Than I Can Handle

Away from you is more than I can handle.

I am lost and wondering aimlessly.

Nothing to ease the lonely.

Just thinking of you constantly.

Flashes of your presence ignite my loneliness

as I disappear into a feeling of lost,

thinking that this too shall pass,

and I wonder at what cost.

These words are not revealing the true meaning of my feel-

ings when I am away from you. Loneliness is that dagger-

like feeling piercing me through and through.

Time moves slowly whenever we are apart

as the night lingers till dawn.

My loneliness and my sleeplessness

only add to the early, empty morn.

Emptiness and a lost feeling can sometimes w

+ + +

96. Devils Have Horns Sometimes Unseen

Devils have horns sometimes unseen

But often evil follows this being

Like an angel with wings outstretched

Disguised as a raven to eat your flesh

When you see the devil without horns

Look for the evil out of the norm

Plain as the appearance would suggest

Look where the evil comes to rest

Evil hides in view of all

Not always recognized, if at all

Hidden in plain view

Like the evil inside of you

Close your eyes but still you see

Evil all around you and me

The devil wants to have its way

But good thoughts ignite each day

Don't be afraid

+ + +

97. Love Is a Delicate Flower

Love is a delicate flower

It opens in its time

It blossom in seasons

Like roses and fine wine

Tender as a kiss

Electric as a storm

Love will find its way

Always true to form

Like a ship sailing on the open sea

The ups and downs are numerous

But slow the pace just a bit

Love can be so glorious

Dreams and fairy tales are fantasy

Like wishing on a star

Love may find you some day

No matter who you are

Love is on the mantle place

Old pictures hung so high

The air that smells like candles

And a companion at your side

+ + +

98. Do Your Thoughts Appear When You Look in the Mirror?

Do your thoughts appear when you look into the mirror,

or do they disappear into the air like vapor?

Do your thoughts appear and disappear

like a sunset through the trees,

or do you smile your favorite smile

and just appear pleased?

Do you look beyond tomorrow

or forever live in the past?

Or is this just a dream,

forced into your heart,

that life has set in motion—

a thought process?

It's hard to guess

how much time is left.

Trust your heart and let it lead you.

Make every moment count.

Happiness can be achieved if you believe

in love and not doubt.

+ + +

99. I Had So Many Chances

I had so many chances

but they all fell apart.

I just hope this time

love will fill my heart.

I tried to come close to you,

tried to make you understand.

I tried to show you my love

and to make future plans.

Each time I have tried before

I failed to make love stay.

Is it me or something else,

or is it a game I unknowingly play?

I have lost my heart before

to many and more.

I would like to think it was not a game,

and this time it's for sure.

Take a chance, maybe you will win.

Nothing ventured, nothing gained.

Throw the dice, sometimes you win.

In the end it's only you to blame.

+ + +

100. My Darling, My Darling

My darling, my darling,

you are missed.

Like your hugs and your kiss.

No matter where I may go,

I see a picture of you

with your lovely glow.

It was only yesterday

that I held you so tight.

Now my arms are empty

on this lonely night.

If I could capture a moment

and freeze it in my mind,

it would be you smiling

and so beautiful all the time.

I am away from you today,

but I am happy inside.

Knowing that your love for me

makes my love for you so alive.

+ + +

101. I Stifled a Tear and Forced a Smile

I stifled a tear and forced a smile

when you said goodbye.

Like a bird you flew away,

and I was left alone to cry.

Sunsets are not the same anymore,

with no beauty and no splendor.

Like a dream gone bad,

I am left alone to ponder.

Many things would pass my way,

and many things I would wonder,

looking for where I went wrong

looking for an answer.

My heart is heavy with sorrow.

My life has no future or plans.

Is my loneliness forever?

I'll never understand.

Hope is eternal,

and life has much purpose.

However things may unfold,

in my thoughts, there would always be us.

+ + +

102. A Journey to Explore the Reality

A journey to explore the reality

A situation based on emotionality

An instinct to assume

That love this time would bloom

Emotional and deceptive

Awaken from similar reactive

Motivated with high expectations

Remembering disappointments

Waiting for the signs to show

Which direction one should go

Is it a game we play

To watch the emotions sway

Changes can inspire changes

We have known this through the ages

But in our hearts we must know

Our love can only grow

Watching the action and reaction

Not overwhelmed with deception

Knowing and believing

Hoping and trusting

Love, oh love, hold my hand, make me understand

Show me signs in our aging times

They say that love would conquer all

Or is that just a fruitless ploy

Love is strong only if it is sound

It can only grow how much, who knows

Truth and trust are its only fodder

When you finally find each another

103. The Mystery of Faith Is No Illusion

The mystery of faith is no illusion.

The mystery of faith is not collusion.

Self-belief and total commitment,

or live a life of utter confusion.

Compassion and charity

are the hands of the mighty.

Eyes that see and a heart that grieves

can only expose the reality.

Believe without a doubt,

and it will determine if you're in or out.

Only from a true heart can you speak,

never from an untrue mouth.

Faith keeps zig-zagging in and out of life.

It's so hard to catch when in flight.

Forgiveness, kindness, truth, and love

can start the sparks that light that light.

Can you lock away faith in a box,

and can it always be there

to take it when you need it,

so everyone can share?

But faith is so elusive

and so very hard to find.

Only the true believers find it

whose hearts are pure and kind.

 + + +

104. Compassion

Compassion

Kindness

Forgiveness

Love

"I love you"

These are words I say every day.

I just want you to know every moment away is lonely and

sad, I must say.

Without you, life would have no meaning

at all.

All would be empty and gray.

I would be destroyed

and totally dismayed.

My life has changed once again,

and I have so much love to give you.

I want to share all my life

and show you how much I need you.

My darling, I want to express my feelings

and show you how much we share.

Each day I say a prayer

for our love to grow, my dear.

The future is so unclear,

and time has a way of its own.

I just want to share

what's left with you and me alone.

You are that angel that touched my life so long ago,

and now you reappeared at my side.

I will treasure your love forever.

Yes, my darling, until I die.

105. I Might Not Be Strong as a Giant

I might not be strong as a giant

or as wise as a guru,

but my thoughts are pure

and my love for you is true.

I have seen many places

and traveled to many lands,

I have had many experiences,

so my love for you I understand.

Away from you can be very lonely.

I would not want to face this world alone.

I am glad we share these feelings.

I can't wait to come back home.

Make no mistake, my darling,

this union was meant to be.

The past was just a rehearsal,

just waiting for you and me.

+ + +

106. I Will Always Remember

I will always remember

your love and thoughtfulness,

the times we shared together,

unbelievable and so precious.

Time is not a factor,

and memories are forever.

I can still see your face,

with its smiles and loving splendor.

Days are long, and nights are longer,

as your memories reappear.

I try to capture all of them

and save them forever.

Tomorrow is another day

as life unfolds.

All that's left are memories

of you for me to hold.

As life continues its journey

and experiences turn into memories,

we hold onto the ones we want

and throw the others to the breeze.

Memories never die;

they are tucked somewhere.

Whenever they are needed,

they will reappear.

107. My Love Is Forever

My love is forever:

This I pledge.

I promise to respect and cherish you

and always look ahead.

Nothing will stand between us.

Tomorrow is a future we still have.

Live life to the fullest;

today is the time we do have.

The past was all that was expected,

with few regrets and many joys.

Today is what counts for us,

and not some useless ploy.

Lean on me and I will learn from you

a thousand things I need to know:

how to make you happy

and how to make us grow.

Yesterday was grand.

Tomorrow will inspire.

Today is a delight.

It's the NOW that lights the fire.

+ + +

108. Every Time I Try to Forget

Every time I try to forget

Your memory keeps pulling me back

The love I shared with you

Is still alive and still new

Time can never erase

And no one can take your place

A make-believe world I still live in

Just wishing and wishing and wishing

A light that shines forever

And never gets dimmer

A love I still remember

Forever and ever

Memories are all that's left

But yet I could never forget

The time we shared together

Would last forever and ever

Memories still linger

I remember your joyful laughter

I see you all around me

So wild, so caring and so free

+ + +

109. Song

There are friends you will have forever

There are friends you lose along the way

Some are friends only in fair weather

Some are friends on stormy days

We spent so many years together

So many friends don't stay close that long

When I think of you, it's laughter I remember

For the sound of you goes through me like a song

Tell me I'll be hearing from you soon

Say I won't have to worry any longer

I'll be patient waiting on your letter

Hoping you are fine and we could find the time to get

together

Friends forever

There are friends taking love for granted

There are friends giving love away

Some are friends that you will find tomorrow

Some are friends from yesterday

Tell me I'll be hearing from you soon

Say I won't have to worry any longer

No matter where you are, I want you to remember

You can always count on me that we will always be best

friends

Friends forever

There are times you take someone for granted

There are times you look the other way

Sometimes your view is slanted

By a friendship gone astray

110. Look Beyond Tomorrow to Find Your Piece of Joy

Look beyond tomorrow to find your piece of joy.

Seek your happiness, and you'll find it's never lost at all.

Make room for disappointments,

but never sway from your goals.

You will find that happiness

before you are very old.

Many obstacles will be in your way

as you travel from day to day.

Gather them like fortune found,

and store them all away.

Make believe you are on a trip

to a far-off exotic land.

Carry all your joyful memories

in your heart and in your hand.

Friends and family are precious;

they are the fuel for the fire.

Let them gather around you

to quench the burning desire.

Joy and happiness are not elusive;

you can find them anywhere.

Look within your inner self.

They were always there.

Hold on to the ones you love;

never let them go.

You will find your true happiness,

and everyone will know.

111. As an Angel Whispers Sweet Songs of Love

As an angel whispers sweet songs of love,

as the water flows gently to the ocean,

in my heart I think of you,

and I promise my full devotion.

You are the angel that makes the music,

that lights the fire of love in me.

You are the glow that sparks the image,

for you are the only angel I see.

You are the stable platform

that I have tied my anchor to.

I am the strength you need

so we both can see it through.

Do not be angry with me, my love,

for my weaknesses are many.

My love for you is the greatest habit,

greater than any.

Like magic, the mystery of affection

is generated by the emotion felt.

My love for you is endless,

so now my life is full of wealth.

+ + +

112. How Can I Tell You What to Sing?

How can I tell you what to sing?

How can I tell you what to think?

You alone can align

what's in your inner mind.

Thoughts are memories returning,

sometimes as a wonderful feeling.

Joy and laughter are a beginning.

Sorrows and sadness are forgetting.

Let your feelings lead your journey.

Life is not a mystery.

Only the truth will set you free.

Love and kindness is the reality.

Give thanks and praises to God

for all the blessings you have been given.

Falling in love each day and a smile

make the joy of the life we are living.

+ + +

113. In My Realm of Solitude

In my realm of solitude,

loneliness is forbidden to enter.

Boundless thoughts are formulated,

articulated in every kind of order—

mastermind by design flaws,

emotional and perplexing,

structured by some unknown sources.

Solitude is awakening and revealing.

Loneliness is self-perpetuating,

lost in a complexity of hope,

while solitude is ever expanding,

to fill the voids and expand the scope.

Energy is wasted on a lonely feeling,

while solitude is a stimulating journey.

Whenever the mind wanders,

the heart is never lonely.

Darkness and the unknown are an entity

which leaves the mind to continue exploring.

Loneliness is an empty feeling,

while solitude is forever expanding.

+ + +

114. I Must Confess I Always Knew

I must confess I always knew

that God has blessed us two.

He has let us share a life together,

a union to last forever.

In our hands he's left us to create

a relationship set in faith.

Honesty, respect and love,

with blessings from above.

Life can take many twists and turns:

happiness, sadness and the unknown.

With your hands in mine, we will discover

we were always meant to be together.

In our senior state, we can contemplate

and leave everything up to faith.

Respect and love for each other

are the key to keeping this miracle together.

+ + +

115. The Future Is Not Far Away

The future is not far away.

Memories are remembered.

A magnet is magnetic.

Labor is work.

You're never late till you get there.

Magic is magical.

A smile is only a smile when it comes from the inside.

It takes at least two to join.

Giving is rewarding.

Love is fertilizer for life.

Kindness in not inbred.

Hot is cool.

Energy is strength.

Happiness is not work.

Thoughts are invisible.

Dreams are theater.

Knowledge is knowing.

Giving freely is kindness.

Only action can show success.

Sharing knowledge is creating life.

+ + +

116. Excuses or Actions

Excuses or actions—

reasons or results—

are our two choices.

We are forced to be vocal

as we lift up our voices.

Objectively we approach the truth

as we examined all the clues.

Excuses are always shadowed

by accomplishments and good news.

A good thought brings a good thought.

A good deed is so rewarding.

A feeling of total respect.

A sense of joy in achieving.

All that glitters is not gold.

A vision can be misunderstood.

What we see sometimes

is just the evil, not the good.

Moving forward without insight,

like looking in the dark without a light.

To fulfill your dreams you must commit.

To win, you must use your wit.

117. It's Not Easy to See the Light

It's not easy to see the light

so early in the morning

when all that's in your sight

is the fog as it is slowing lifting.

Like magic, the light changes

into a golden amber glow

and lingers just to let the day unfold

into life's continuous flow.

Forward in all our journey from day to day,

we see what we are supposed to see,

what appears to be reality.

The truth is what it will always be.

Tolerance is not attained without practice.

Seeing the other side in not easy.

Sometimes blinded by ignorance,

our vision is sometimes cloudy.

To give is an action worth taking.

A kindness given to others is rewarding.

There is no need for thanking

when you're freely giving.

Space and time are endless,

like a dream going on forever,

never ending, just repeating,

forever and ever.

Memories are thoughts.

118. Watching the Cherry Blossoms

Watching the cherry blossoms

blooming as spring unfolds,

overwhelmed with its beauty,

a beauty to behold.

Abundant and colorful they bloom,

displaying their changing hues.

A gift sent from heaven,

with their red, pink and blues.

Spreading out its branches and fragrance,

its beauty surrounds us all.

Beginning in the warmth of summer,

but disappearing at the start of fall.

As the winter months approach,

the cherry trees are bare.

They stand firm as centurions,

waiting for the spring each year.

+ + +

119. I See Them Moving To and Fro

I see them moving to and fro

I see the need and greed

I watch with reflective eyes

I see the fear that feeds the need

I see faces with many expressions

I see the silence of space expands

I see many different people

From many foreign lands

I see darkness off in the distance

I see smiling children playing

I see life from its beginning

The living without giving

The window of my vision

Is enough to realize

What I see is not an illusion

But reality of the unwise

I am sitting on this corner

Of 19th and Stout, wondering

What's it about

People moving in all direction

Driven by habit or emotion and doubt

Looking deep inside my thoughts

I finally realized

Each action is pointless

Without a reaction to materialize

120. Things We Worry About Seldom Ever Matter

Things we worry about seldom ever matter.

Fear of the unknown is often shattered.

A thought that persists in negativity

is often not the reality.

Memories are the foundation of experience,

acquired by remembering its elegance.

Positive thoughts are uplifting;

they can replace the not knowing.

Dangers are not always seen visually,

hidden and disguised so eloquently.

Unraveling and analyzing the situation

can often reveal the solution.

Fear not, for fear is just an emotion,

controlled by many notions.

Only from within you'll gather

the answers to all that matters.

+ + +

121. Day by Day You Pass My Way

Day by day you pass my way.

I see you from my window.

You look so distant and afraid,

hiding behind that shadow.

I try to understand your plight.

I cannot seem to follow.

Your face is so distressed,

burdened by your sorrow.

Depression, heavy on your shoulder,

the weight is unbearable.

Your motion is distorted.

It carries you as in a cradle.

Elevate is an option

not easy to achieve.

Believing in your vulnerability

relives that fear you weave.

Hopelessness and negativity

must never be the goal.

All things can be achieved

as your precious life unfolds.

+ + +

122. I Talked to God Today

I talked to God today

and asked for his love.

A gentle breeze touched my face,

sent from up above.

I spoke to God again today

to take away my sorrow.

He blessed me once again

by giving me tomorrow.

I spoke to God today

to give him thanks and praise.

He smiled on me once more

and blessed me with his grace.

I talked to God today

and asked for his blessings.

He answered me once again

with health and all its dressings.

I talked to God today

just to let him know

for all that he has given me,

I am grateful, and it shows.

I talked to God today

and asked him for a favor:

to let our love together

grow stronger and stronger.

I talked to God today

to strengthen my faith.

He gave me understanding

and the patience to wait.

+ + +

123. I Stop and Talk to People on the Way

I stop and talk to people on the way.

I listen to what they have to say.

I try to understand their plight.

I tell them never give up the fight.

I see the suffering and pain.

I always try to explain.

Life is not endless, I confess.

You take the bad with the best.

When you awake to face the day,

thank God for yesterday.

All your troubles won't go away;

the prayers you say could show the way.

Give a smile to all you meet.

Wish all the best to all you greet.

Touch everyone you meet with kindness, for kindness is

godliness.

Greet everyone with love not hate.

Show them the strength of your faith.

Give them hope and guidance.

Share your love, not your silence.

+ + +

124. The Hate That One Sparks

The hate that one sparks

is like a dagger in the dark.

It never lets you see it,

because it's hidden in the deepest.

The shadow that is cast

is like a massive mast.

Under disguise it hides,

like a thief in the night.

Truth and honesty are not blinded

behind walls of security well guarded.

Everything hidden out of sight

would one day come to light.

The inner cannot hide forever.

Like the opening to life as a flower,

the true image will be revealed,

on your face or in a whisper.

Truth is like a beacon or a key.

Its presence is there to set you free.

The path you choose is your answer

that sets the foundation for the future.

+ + +

125. The Only Links to the Past Are Memories and Dreams

The only links to the past are memories and dreams,

triggered by pictures and thoughts, it seems.

A flashback that sparks a moment

brings back that special event like a familiar scent.

A face shadowed and aged by time.

A moment shared by a friend.

A word spoken in kindness.

A remembrance from way back when.

A thought that time can't erase.

A recollection in time and space.

A joyous laugh in an echo.

A remembrance we will forever know.

A spike that laid a foundation,

lost in the whirlwind of emotions.

Sparking the memories of happiness.

Mixed with a feeling of loneliness.

Printed in our minds like a photo,

forever it lingers and glows,

to be collected and reviewed,

anytime and anywhere we go.

126. She Could Not Turn Straw into Gold

She could not turn straw into gold.

They came from afar to save her soul

They talked about the times to come

when all that was achieved will be undone.

Believing in what her heart is told

will soon be revealed and unfold.

Light that shines to show the way

with promise of a brand new day.

Try if you must to believe her plight.

Doubts and questions she saw in her sight.

Salvation or redemption is so vague

from what is lost and what is gained.

Firm is her belief in good;

All her devotion misunderstood.

Faith is so hard to hold and grow,

Forever dancing to and fro.

127. It Is Not What You Think It Is

It is not what you think it is.

Don't be fooled by its appearance,

disgusted as an angel

but revealed as innocence.

Blind dreams are sometimes blinded.

By not looking at all the angles, we see.

What's hidden in plain view

will be revealed eventually.

Shadows do not hide the obvious.

It's there for all to see.

But the shadow hides the darkness

from all who will not see.

Nothing can be overshadowed by

coverings up of the past.

Truth will reveal everything

when the truth is from the heart.

A feeling of joy and an expression of laughter

can brighten up any day.

Joy can turn to laughter

or turn the other way.

+ + +

128. Sitting and Drinking in the Air

Sitting and drinking in the air,

watching the sun disappear,

feeling the wind kissing my face,

gently perfuming the air with its grace.

Thoughts flash with lighting speed

from one thing to the other.

Flashbacks fill my mind once more.

I think of you, MYAH, my love, no other.

I think of what could have been

if we had only stayed the course awhile.

The world would be at our feet,

and stars would be our guide,

looking for answers never to be found.

Life turned out its own way.

Ships that pass in the night

would love again someday.

Shadow of memories dance in my head

like a sparrow taking honey from a flower.

Music and vistas trigger new awakening:

memories I'll always treasure.

+ + +

129. Informed with Knowledge

Informed with knowledge,

but not understanding it.

To stand on a principle or illusion

is not the answer or solution, I admit.

Set in your mind a strong imprint,

believing all blindly without doubt.

Principles set without true facts,

oblivious to what's it all about.

Unaware of your surroundings,

like believing without reasoning.

A blind eye to all around you

will lead to your ultimate failings.

Awake thoughts of inner self

modify principles with truth.

New ideas can lift your spirits

and bring forward abundant fruits.

A closed mind is not productive;

there's little room for change.

Believing in something unequivocally

sometimes leads to the insane.

+ + +

130. I See the Mountains before Me

I see the mountains before me,

the fragrance of flowers kissed by the spring's rain.

I see the valley and the treetops

as I travel through this rugged terrain.

It appears to me so euphoric

and yet so surreal.

The landscape before me

would one day be concrete and steel.

My mind wonders as to its beginnings,

with its savannas, rivers and plains,

with its wildlife inhabitants,

wandering in the torrential rains.

The beauty that surrounds me

is sacred and it's old.

The snowcap in the distance

paints a picture to behold.

I embrace the feeling of belonging

and a strong urge to protect.

The world of progress is fast approaching,

a memory in retrospect.

All I see before me

is raped and plundered by man

in the name of progress and modernization,

while muffling the cries of the land.

131. Expectations and Reality

Expectations and reality:

the height of vanity.

Not knowing your self-worth

is not knowing the reality.

Look beyond tomorrow.

Expect nothing to be real.

Open your eyes to reality.

Accept all in the way you feel.

Your sight can be fooled

by painted images and icons,

but the truth can only be found

inside yourself and not beyond.

Reality is in your eyesight

as plain as the light of day.

Don't let your expectations fool you;

don't let them lead you astray.

Being true to one's self

is a rule you should always live by,

Take nothing for granted,

and separate the truth from lies.

+ + +

132. You Are My Life and My Salvation

You are my life and my salvation.

I wanted you to know.

You give me all I need

as my love for you grows.

You are my Rock of Gibraltar,

Standing tall and strong.

I hold on to you for strength,

and nothing can go wrong.

You inspire my every existence.

You encourage my every mood.

You are the one I look up to;

Your love is like a food.

I thank God each day for you

as I watch our love expand.

I am so proud of you, my dear,

as we share this life and make plans.

There is so much more I want to say.

Your kindness and your smiles—

I can find so many things to praise,

like the love light in your eyes.

I thank you for the ride,

for one day this journey will end.

I thank God for giving me you,

as a lover and a friend.

133. Is It Real or Surreal?

Is it real or surreal?

Is it fate or is it faith?

Is it known or unknown?

Is it late or not too late?

Live life—

like a flowing spring,

like a bird in flight,

soaring in the wind

to the top of a mountain

high above the mist,

almost touching the stars,

wanting to kiss.

Another day is dawning—

like milk and honey flowing,

a blessing from above,

from God the all-knowing.

Memories are not magical.

They appear to be so real.

They keep coming back.

They continue, like a wheel.

Look beyond tomorrow.

The future has its plans.

It will reveal all soon enough,

so all can understand.

134. On This Empty Piece of Paper

On this empty piece of paper,

I want to write a song for you,

to tell you my desires

and to pledge my love that's true.

I wake up every morning

knowing you are there.

A light shines within me;

you're my morning prayer.

My day is filled with joy.

Your smiles brighten the day.

You light up my life like a flame.

It's you and I, come what may.

My dreams are fulfilled.

My heart is satisfied,

knowing that you will share

these feelings, you and I.

As the day goes on,

I have so much love to share,

just knowing that you love me.

I promise to always be there.

+ + +

135. Knowledge Is the Greatest Gift

Knowledge is the greatest gift

that man can give to man,

simply by teaching

so all can understand.

The receiving of knowledge—

a possession for a lifetime,

free to share with anyone,

anywhere or anytime.

As knowledge is forever growing,

as mankind is evolving,

all would get the message

by sharing and teaching.

Knowledge is not heavy.

It is carried in your head.

Once it is acquired,

it is yours until you're dead.

Acquiring knowledge and keeping it

is selfish and immature.

Knowledge built on knowledge

is forever growing more and more.

Faith, attitude and consciousness

are all generated by the self.

Life will be wasted

if the only thoughts are for wealth.

Happiness isn't measured by possessions,

nor is it measured by gold.

Happiness can only be found

deep down in your inner soul.

A smile given from the surface

can brighten the darkest room.

The radiance generated internally

is like a flower in full bloom.

+ + +

136. My Thoughts Are Full of Love for You

My thoughts are full of love for you

as the dawn morphs into morning.

I picture your beautiful face,

and my joy is overwhelming.

Time puts things in perspective.

But when I am in the moment,

my thoughts are amplified.

I can feel and smell your presence.

Light will turn to darkness

as the day turns into night.

My devotion to you, my love,

is like an everlasting light.

Things will change and time will pass,

and new things will be altered.

But my feelings for you, my love,

Will never, ever falter.

You are the joy that love brings,

like a warm breeze on a winter morning.

Your love wraps around me

like a blanket of happy feelings.

+ + +

137. Can You Feel the Sorrow?

Can you feel the sorrow,

thinking there's no tomorrow?

Hope is eternal,

but is death the final?

Where is the future.

without danger?

Every day is a trial.

Would today be the final?

With no vision

we make decisions.

Without the facts

we react.

Believing the unknown,

acting alone,

no rhyme or reason,

we ignore the allegations.

Take time to study

what can really happen.

Without the plan,

you cannot stand.

There are solutions.

There are conclusions.

Without hope, they say,

there's always a prayer.

+ + +

138. Like It Was Long Ago

Like it was long ago,

what was mine was yours also.

Remember the past.

It's disappearing fast.

Memories are fading

as life is changing,

like a flash of light

disappearing from sight.

Comrades and friends

sadly are at their end.

Someone to lean on

is already gone.

It's disappointing

not knowing

who is on the attack

or who has your back.

Like an intrusion,

it's a delusion.

Is trust in a friend ending,

or is it an ending of trusting?

+ + +

139. There Are Consequences

There are consequences

in putting up fences.

The ones you lock out

are full of fear and doubts.

The walls you build to keep you in—

make them strong and not too thin,

for those you want to keep out

will never know what's it about.

Your motives would be misunderstood,

though you tried to explain all you could.

Walls built to restrict the friendly

can also let in the enemy.

You cannot live in this world alone,

like a hermit sitting on a stone.

The breeze that blows touches everyone,

and the warmth of the sun misses no one.

Break down your barricades,

and come awake for your sake.

Welcome all to participate.

Life is love not hate.

Keep all you love close to you.

Provide a shelter for all, not the few.

The rewards you will achieve

will be the love that you weave.

140. It's a Pity to Have Apathy

It's a pity to have apathy

for the depressed or witty.

No feelings for the downtrodden—

or is it Armageddon?

Emotional and distraught,

in a whirlwind of thoughts.

The forgotten souls

with their stories untold.

Flashes of existence and hope,

mixed up with its enormity and scope.

The mind and rights are erased

and left with an empty space.

What will be a solution—

sedition or a forum or a union?

Scattered like sand after a sandstorm,

few are willing to pursue the norm.

What would be the answer—

a continued discussion and banter?

Should we as one make a stand

and formulate a Godly plan?

Faith and hope should be a guide,

forgetting all the promises and lies.

A solid ground to stand firm,

demanding what's honestly earned.

141. You Worked Hard to Achieve What You Have

You worked hard to achieve what you have.

But you must work harder to achieve

what you desire.

Nothing comes easy in life,

no matter how much you acquire.

Little things are easy to achieve,

like compassion, kindness and charity.

Being the person you want to be

can be accomplished easily.

Stand firm for what you believe in.

Never accept what you think is unfair.

Look beyond the facts and opinions.

Examine all in order to be fair.

All can be achieved

with a little effort and pain.

A firm determination

is all that's needed to light the flames.

Never give up as long as you have life,

the most precious gift you were given.

There is so much to be achieved

before we get to heaven.

Material wealth is no wealth at all;

it can disappear in a moment.

Doing good and helping others

are the riches you would have in the end.

+ + +

142. Forgetting How to Forgive

Forgetting how to forgive

is forgetting how to live.

Never ever forget,

but learn without regrets.

Scars are left, but they will heal,

they will melt like butter or steel.

Learn by throwing hate away.

Let love and forgiveness stay.

Carry your burdens one by one.

Most are not heavy, only some.

Heavy is the weight of hate,

but forgiveness is the power of faith.

Magical, like a shadow disappearing,

forgiveness is as easy as forgiving.

Learning by experience and time

can only be enlightened by being kind.

Look the other way and let go;

by not forgetting, you will know.

Forgiving is lifting the burden forever—

a weight you will no longer carry ever.

+ + +

143. I Watch the River Flow

I watch the river flow,

going to and fro.

I see the ripples dance

like fairies in a trance.

I walk along its banks,

admiring the display.

Meandering in its flow,

heading for the bay,

with profound efficiency,

the river winds away

with determination and purpose.

Nothing stands in its way.

Its shallows and its depths

make boundaries without respect,

changing courses as it goes,

with its abundance and overflow.

The beauty as it winds

through the meadows and the vines—

the sounds that it makes

is the music it creates.

Nothing stands in its way,

be it night or be it day.

It will maintain its flow

as this mighty river grows.

144. All Around Me I See Sorrow

All around me I see sorrow

with no hope for tomorrow.

Tears and hopelessness surround me,

a cry for help and sympathy.

The hunger in the faces of the children

is visual and not hidden.

The storm has destroyed their homes

and left them wandering all alone.

Yesterday, when hope was in the air,

all was provided and the future clear.

Fortune has turned its back on them;

all that's left is destruction and mayhem.

Wandering aimlessly without hope,

almost at the end of the rope.

Where and who to turn to?

Where to go and what to do?

Open your heart and find a space

to bring a smile to just one face.

Nothing is hopeless and unfixable;

anything and everything is possible.

Turning their eyes toward the sky,

asking God to explain why.

Trust in God, and they'll see why.

He will provide for all who cry.

145. I Understand the Reason the Music Has to Play

I understand the reason the music has to play:

to drive away the evil

that lingers and wants to stay.

The rhythm and the melody

make a true song, they say.

But the lyrics and the meter

complete the whole array.

Mixed with good feeling,

the story that it tells

can lighten up your spirit

and make your heart excel.

Sounds that the instruments make

are generated by the players.

But the feelings of the song

are delivered from the inner.

Music is a force that cannot be seen,

so powerful to our emotional feel.

The mood is set and memories awaken,

and all ill will is soon forgotten.

Sing and dance—let your heart be free—

awaken the emotions, and you'll see.

Your life will have more laughter,

and none of your worrying will matter.

Music is good for the soul,

more valuable than diamonds or gold.

A melody that lingers in your head

can soothe emotions, giving joy instead.

146. As the Day Passes and the Sunset Is on the Horizon

As the day passes and the sunset is on the horizon,

as the clouds drift across the sky,

as the birds catch fish as they fly,

I sit here with tears of joy in my eyes.

How do I send that much love so far?

No carrier can hold these feelings.

But I will send them little by little,

until your cup is overflowing.

Missing you says so little,

not conveying what I truly mean.

Like trying to kiss your favorite girl

through a window screen.

+ + +

147. Box Up Your Thoughts

Box up your thoughts.

Bottle your laughter.

Grab love.

Pack up memories that matter.

Don't cover happy.

Don't give up the quest

Don't neglect your brother's need.

Don't mistake the worst as the best.

Feelings do matter in the end

to make a dramatic change.

What is felt in your heart

will lead you once again.

Let the wind blow, let the rain fall.

Let's all join in the celebration.

A new adventure is about to begin

with old and new creations.

Run with me, for walking is too slow.

There is so much road to cover.

Hold my hand, and together,

we will travel this journey forever.

+ + +

148. What Does a Bird Feel in Flight?

What does a bird feel in flight?

What does the water feel flowing over the rock?

What does the wind feel hurrying by—

is it destiny or is it luck?

The voice of the forest asked loudly,

Is there an explanation to this?

And a voice in a quiet tone replied,

This was meant to be; it's my wish.

Like time goes forward always,

and reliable as the setting sun;

like the joy of being in love

and being loved by someone.

What good fortune needs explaining,

like the gift of love that's true,

or the sweet smell of jasmine in bloom?

I am so glad it is you.

+ + +

149. Do Not Doubt My Love for You, My Dear

Do not doubt my love for you, my dear.

It shows in many ways,

like smiles on my face and joy in my heart,

and thoughts of you all day.

You being my first love—

I stored it all away.

And now that I found you again,

love came flooding down my way.

How do you describe love?

It's very hard to say.

Is it a feeling,

or is it a warmth that never goes away?

$+\ +\ +$

150. Light a Fire. Watch It Burn.

Light a fire. Watch it burn.

Watch the waves take their turn.

See the moon disappear each day.

Wait for the sunset as it fades away.

Dancing lights set the mood

where everything is understood.

Sparks that fly into the sky

make a sparkle in your eyes.

The first light that illuminates your face

is impressed by your grace.

As the sun spreads its joy around,

you, the queen, must wear the crown.

Don't take for granted what's gifted to you

count all p

151. Come Travel with Me and See

Come travel with me and see

the wonder that's out there,

like mountains covered with mystery,

and costumes they wear at the fair.

Over oceans and rivers alike,

over desert and forests too,

together we will share a love

just meant for me and you.

No walls would be our barrier.

No negativity would keep us back.

"Forward" would be our motto,

always on the attack.

Where dreams become reality

and all our wishes are fulfilled,

and smiles are in our hearts

as our love grows stronger still.

Come hold my hand. Let's wander

through all there is to see.

Let's take with us this loving gift

wherever we may be.

+ + +

152. I Feel Like a Fluttering Bird

I feel like a fluttering bird

trying to dry its wings,

thinking how to live my life,

unclear of what the future brings.

Hope is on the horizon.

Reality is yet to be seen.

Time for us was never a factor

for a love born in our teens.

You said I was your first love.

I felt that same way too.

Now that we found each other again,

there is so much left to do.

+ + +

153. Put Your Abilities Ahead of Your Fears

Put your abilities ahead of your fears.

It is only you who care.

Reach for heights seldom attained:

nothing ventured, nothing gained.

Like smoke disappears in the air,

face each day without a care.

A good deed done today

will be the inspiration to light the way.

Make every day count like it's the last.

Make the present outdo the past.

Keep a peaceful and open mind,

and all good things you will find.

154. Draw Attention Away from the Senses

Draw attention away from the senses,

so as to calm the mind.

Think of all the circumstances,

and an answer you will find.

Decisions made in haste

are not always a solid choice.

But there's no time to waste

if you have heard the right voice.

A wish is not a dream come true,

nor is it a fulfillment of a desire.

Led by emotions in overview,

It's our love that lights the fire.

I am yours and you are mine—

a love made in heaven.

Like the creation of fine wine,

we were lucky to be chosen.

+ + +

155. The Warmth of a Shadow

The warmth of a shadow

The reality of pretense

The ocean of nothingness

A blind man's vision

The color of thought

The light of darkness

The imagination of reality

The lonely of helplessness

A flower that stuns its beauty

A promise never broken

A feeling without emotion

A hateful word not spoken

Silence has no regrets

Like words spoken in haste

Love is like a symphony

Its music blankets every space

+ + +

156. If the Truths Be Told

If the truths be told

as the story unfolds,

the start of the killing

was just the beginning.

The men not expecting

that something was brewing,

they gathered not knowing,

not contemplating a killing.

To protect this land,

they had to make a stand.

They never wanted a fight,

not knowing the plight.

A gloom was in the air,

thick with violence and despair.

No bargains to make,

it was a horrid mistake.

They knew it was wrong

to hold onto sacred ground.

The stage was all set.

The men had no regrets.

Many had died

not knowing why.

The land that was gained

had claimed so much pain.

No one survived.

Only the mothers cried.

Whatever was gained

was in the mind of the insane.

Death was in the air

when the smoke had cleared.

The land that was won

belonged to no one.

Fighting for land,

no way to understand,

nothing was gained.

The land remains unclaimed.

Who had won? At what a cost?

All had died. Oh, what a loss.

What was done

can never be undone.

What is sacred land?

Why did they make a stand?

It's only a piece of ground

that's always been around.

Few will remember

who died in the plunder.

Their lives will be remembered.

All had perished. None surrendered.

+ + +

157. Take Time Out to Say Things That Please Others

Take time out to say things that please others.

Don't be afraid to express your true emotions.

Someday they will be understood and practiced,

regardless of their disguise as a solution.

Aim high, and greater heights will be achieved.

Sometimes losses can be turned into successes.

A mountain is never too high to climb.

Achievements count—not misses.

Try to match the color of the wind.

Try to grab and hold the sun.

I know in my heart that you are

now the one and only one.

In a flashback I saw your face again,

like a beacon guiding me there.

No longer do I fear the outcome,

for the future holds no despair.

158. I See a Fountain of Petals Scattering across the Countryside

I see a fountain of petals scattering across the countryside.

I see the wind swirling, trying to catch and rebuild every

flower.

What a beautiful bouquet it has assembled—

prominent and a masterpiece like no other.

You are that flower.

Your beauty is not for self but for others.

You are the flower,

like no other.

Smells of sweet jasmine and roses linger about.

Your scent penetrates, and your fragrance fills the air.

Your presence makes all things better,

with a bit of your pomp and flair.

You are the flower.

Your beauty is not for you but others.

You are the flower,

like no other.

You are that flower

I promise to always treasure.

Forever and ever—

our love for each other.

159. Why Do I Remember All the Lonely Nights without You?

Why do I remember all the lonely nights without you?

They linger in my head as if to punish me.

I try to think of happy times

when I was young and fancy free.

My thoughts keep going back to the past,

like a magnet pulling with great force.

I think of time that was lost and

how life took me on a different course.

I am thankful and give praises every day

For being able to find my true love and soul mate.

Is it a streak of good fortune

or a love that God created?

160. Not Knowing What I Would Find

Not knowing what I would find,

I was anxious to know your heart.

I found you were just as beautiful as ever

after so many years apart.

We remembered many things of long ago.

Some were joyous, and some were sad.

Your smile and kindness haven't changed,

kindled by the fire in your heart.

Stolen moments with you once again—

nothing has changed except time.

Those feelings that were hidden away

might surface anytime.

+ + +

161. In My Lifetime I Feel Cheated. There's Not Enough Time for Loving . . .

In my lifetime I feel cheated. There's not enough time for

loving you, my all.

My time with you is precious and valuable

and could not be measured at all.

A feeling that is invincible,

a thought of being alone till eternity.

A life that's left to wither and die

somehow survives and is me.

A wondering thought that amplified this

emotion and distorts the facts

can only explain the solution as a

function that finds itself transformed into that.

+ + +

162. So Innocent You Lay There Sleeping

So innocent you lay there sleeping,

like a baby dreaming.

What a sight to behold,

so at peace with all the world.

I want you to wake up smiling

from a dream that's revealing.

Sharing my love with you

morphed into a lover's brew.

I watch you open your eyes

when all sleep died.

Your first sight you see is me,

waiting to share life's ecstasies.

163. Play a Song and Dance Awhile

Play a song and dance awhile.

Light the room up with your smile.

Stay a little longer and talk to me.

There's nowhere else I would rather be.

You made a mark upon my heart.

I somehow knew it from the start.

It took awhile to see the light.

But now I know that I was right.

I never took the time to say,

I've always loved you since that day.

With the intervention from above,

I can finally show you my love.

+ + +

164. Where Are You, My Dearest?

Where are you, my dearest?

I am like a child without its mother.

I am lost without your presence,

Like a man without his lover.

Time is moving so slowly,

Like a river up a hill.

I think of you constantly,

Like I never knew I will.

Come back to me quickly.

Please do not delay.

And make all things complete.

And make it stay that way.

I never knew you were my soul mate.

I knew you were my friend.

I should've known a long time ago,

We'd be together again.

My heart is sad; there are tears in my eyes.

All I do is whine.

I miss your warm and tender body

Cuddling next to mine.

+ + +

165. Leonardo Was Making Art and Science a Fusion

Leonardo was making art and science a fusion.

Gandhi was about peace not illusion.

Each day that passes,

We see the changes to our lives on our faces.

Make a plan, take stand.

Never surrender.

Never go under.

You are the inventor.

You are the maker.

You are the master

Of what you create.

Make a plan, take a stand.

Never surrender.

Never go under.

Take nothing for granted.

Nothing is cemented.

There're so many changes.

Sometimes for nothing.

+ + +

166. Time and Other Factors

Time and other factors

couldn't end our reunion.

Our coming back together

was divine intervention.

As we go through living

and life's experiences unfold,

the love we have for each other

was never getting old.

Once again reunited,

just like a fairy tale.

This coming of us together,

a love that never failed.

+ + +

167. What Can I Say? It's Another Day without You

What can I say? It's another day without you.

The sky's gray, the mood is blue.

All I can do

is think of you.

This loneliness: it's you who I miss.

Your love and your kiss

are why I exist.

I know that it shows.

I am about to explode.

I alone know

how much you are missed.

I'll try not to cry. I'll dry the tears from my eyes.

Only God knows why

this love has survived.

+ + +

168. My Life's Rehearsal Was for Your Affection

My life's rehearsal was for your affection,

Not knowing how things might unfold.

Responsibility took us in many directions,

But at last we have a goal.

Your name and a number written on a piece of paper,

Sitting on my desk collecting dust.

I looked at it countless times,

Wondering if I should call or not.

The time was right to make the call

That renewed that hidden spark.

Our love can only grow from here—

The bringing together of two hearts.

Your response to me was so sweet,

I will always remember.

I laughed out loud and jumped for joy.

From then on my life got better.

What has passed is gone

To some another place forever.

Only you and I remain,

To always be together.

What I felt in the past

Was not of the heart.

I kept fooling myself,

Right from the very start.

+ + +

169. Give of Yourself So Others May Live

Give of yourself so others may live,

Generously sharing all you can give.

Pain and sorrow can wait till tomorrow.

Today is the day that life begins.

All of yesterday was only a dream.

Today is all that's left, so it seems.

Tomorrow will surely follow today

With hope, love and joy, we pray.

A lifetime is not sufficient

To experience all one can,

Sharing life's adventures

So others can understand.

+ + +

170. My Impatience Is Getting the Better of Me

My impatience is getting the better of me,

While tearing me apart.

I just can't wait

To touch your hand and share what's in my heart.

Distance and time will come together again.

Like the rivers and the sea.

Then once again we will embrace,

And what will be will be.

It just appears that the days get longer

When I'm away from you.

Each time we get together,

I fall in love anew.

+ + +

171. Thoughts of You Fill My Head

Thoughts of you fill my head

With a warm and fuzzy feeling.

In my empty house I think of you,

While staring at the ceiling.

I miss your smile and burning laughter

Whenever we are not together.

My thoughts are of you only,

No one else really matters.

Missing you is sad and disturbing,

With thoughts of loneliness and depression.

All my love I will give to you.

My heart is your possession.

+ + +

172. You Have Always Been a Part of Me

You have always been a part of me.

I was so blind not to see.

Now that I look back in retrospect,

This love was eventually meant to be.

Time has served us well, my dear,

By giving us both joy and happiness.

Those special people in our lives

Can only add to our togetherness.

I should never have let you go,

No matter what you said to me.

But the past has made the present possible,

Or our love would never be.

Regrets are sometimes useless thoughts.

+ + +

173. Like a Dream That Fades into a Memory

Like a dream that fades into a memory,

Like the sand that scatters across the lonely desert,

My time with you fades faster and faster

With every joyful minute.

I will cherish this rendezvous

Like a prize in my pocket,

Touching it from time to time

Like a toy ship or a rocket.

Goodbyes are hard to say,

Full of tears and sorrow.

Lucky for some of us,

There's always a tomorrow.

174. Questions without Answers

Questions without answers

Are like a dancers without a partner,

A song without a melody,

Or music without harmony.

A heart happy and content,

Not searching for anything.

Peaceful time in the morning,

Emotions overflowing.

Stop and smell the roses

As you pass along the way.

Never forget the message

That love will find its way.

+ + +

175. Saying I Love You Is Not Saying Enough

Saying I love you is not saying enough.

Saying I need you is not saying that much.

But what I'm saying is that I want you

And can't wait for your touch.

Wishing for a miracle,

Just to see you by my side.

Wishing with all my heart

To keep you satisfied.

I keep seeing you appear and disappear

As in a tantalizing dream.

I reached out and held you,

While this dream appeared so real.

+ + +

176. The Days Seem Longer without You

The days seem longer without you,

So empty and alone.

I count the minutes apart,

While sending love notes on my phone.

I anxiously wait for your answer,

To see what you may say.

Sometimes I am so impatient

To send my love your way.

You are all I think about

During my daily chores.

I think of you all the time,

Now even more and more.

+ + +

177. Making Wishes and Dreaming of You

Making wishes and dreaming of you

Is all I do all day.

Remembering things I always knew,

Now you're back in my life to stay.

I count my blessings each morning

And thank god up above.

I am so happy that you are willing

To share your precious love.

I will never disappoint your expectations.

I will try to live up to all your wishes.

It will be my one satisfaction

To shower you with my kisses.

+ + +

178. Help Me to Live

Help me to live

Help me to give too

All the love I possess

I'll gladly give you

Walk in the shadows

Avoiding the light

Cover your eyes

Hidden in plain sight

Leaving can be sad

So dry your eyes

There will be more days

To enjoy your smiles

+ + +

179. No Matter How Hard I Try

No matter how hard I try,

I can't explain this feeling.

Words cannot express

The hurting or the healing.

This pain apart that hurt my heart

Will go away someday.

With you in my arms engulfed in your charms,

Our future is whatever we say.

I count the days we are apart,

So lonely and so boring.

I want to feel you at my side

When I wake up in the morning.

+ + +

180. This Distance That Rips Apart My Heart

This distance that rips apart my heart,

That keeps us apart, I despise.

I searched my mind to try and find,

Some kind of compromise.

I reach out for you, but you're not there.

I cannot show you that I care.

Then sadness falls as I recall

From this distance that we share.

I will build myself a time machine,

So I can instantly be at your side,

And never ever surrender again,

To the hurt that tears my eyes.

181. I Want to Create New Memories for You

I want to create new memories for you.

I want you to have new experiences.

I want you to be all you want to be.

These would be my wishes.

With you by my side

And the world before us,

There is only our success,

Powered by our love and trust.

Something divine has brought us together again,

And I thank god for that.

You are that special lady,

To bring it all back.

+ + +

182. Words That Are Said Are from the Heart

Words that are said are from the heart,

Spoken with thoughts of affection.

Love and trust are what we share,

Understanding without a question.

Deeds that show your personality

Can clearly be seen.

A touch of your presence

Only brightens the scene.

You are like a flower that is a joy to all,

With your bright and free spirit.

Your happiness is paramount.

Together we can enjoy all of it.

183. Like a Ship Adrift in the Ocean

Like a ship adrift in the ocean,

Lost and without direction,

Looking for any signs of land,

Trying to make some kind of plan.

Hold my hand. Stand by my side.

Never accept a compromise.

Looking forward, never back,

It's not as clear as white or black.

What the future brings, we never know.

Be not afraid of friend nor foe.

No one can destroy a true feeling,

Like our friendship made in heaven.

Time reveals for all to see.

Nothing hidden between you and me.

As clear as light, it's plain to see,

In the end it's only you and me.

Make a wish and see it come true.

It will surprise even you.

+ + +

184. I Am Captivated by Your Charm

I am captivated by your charm.

I am impressed by your togetherness.

When I'm your arms,

I'm in a world of total bliss.

Your touch is like a fire

That lights my inner self.

It is my desire

To love you and no one else.

Do not worry, my darling,

I'll always be here for you.

Our first love is again blossoming,

And that is overdue.

+ + +

185. Myah

Like lost treasures found in the sands of time,

You have returned to me in the end.

I am lost and confused, even amused,

That I am so lucky to have you as a friend.

Your beauty shines through like a beacon.

Your laughter and smile are so infectious.

Your warmth and kindness I admire.

Your presence lifts all of us.

My thoughts include you now

In every imaginable plan.

I try to dismiss them as fantasy or dreams

But I never can.

+ + +

186. I Hitched a Ride on the Wind

I hitched a ride on the wind

as it traveled through the mountains and valleys.

I saw the brooks and rivers

as they wound their way along the alleys.

The wind lifted me above the clouds

as I bathed in the cool mist.

I could see the ocean in the distance

and the meadows in total bliss.

I soared among the tall trees

as the wind carried me high.

I saw the rivers and ocean glittering

like diamonds in the sky.

The ride was invigorating.

We silently moved among the towns,

gently touching the rooftops,

as we headed to the desert grounds.

The warmth of the sun heated the breeze

as we kissed the loose desert sand.

The whirlwind created a sandstorm

that engulfed the parched land.

As the wind was twisting and twirling,

I hung on tight to my imagination.

My eyes could see the spectacle

and all of God's creation.

+ + +

187. My Mind Keeps Drifting

My mind keeps drifting

in and out of reality.

Like a ship adrift

in an open sea.

I tried to harness my thoughts

into a pleasant place,

but the constant vacillation

makes my thoughts a waste.

How can I harness my ideas

when I cannot contain their course,

looking for a solution

in this mind that I have lost?

Insanity—or is it delusional?—

to think with a broken mind.

Solutions are so vague and complex,

while the truth is hard to find.

Take some time to collect my thoughts

and construct a concrete plan.

Try to formulate a genuine solution

while trying to understand.

In a state of tranquility,

the dying search for reality.

The mind is left to rejuvenate

by trusting in God with faith.

+ + +

188. Stand Firm for Your Ideologies

Stand firm for your ideologies.

Leave no room for compromise,

no matter the consequences.

Care not who lives or dies.

Self is paramount in your thinking.

Your fellow man is of no importance.

Seeing things from only one direction.

Showing all your selfish ignorance.

A chronicle of worldly thoughts,

condensed into worthless ideals.

Wrongful acts of suppression,

continuous as the perpetual wheel.

No quarters given.

No hope for the victimized.

A hopelessness that forms a pattern,

Led to slaughter with open eyes.

There cannot be a conscience

when thoughts are only of self,

when the mind is so corrupt,

and the goal the accumulation of wealth.

Policy and politics are synonymous.

Their rules are not negotiated

but are applied to the masses,

wherever and whenever needed.

+ + +

189. Each Day We Live Is Precious

Each day we live is precious.

Each life we touch is glorious.

Let the day be full of laughter,

and enjoy the joys we gather.

Face the day with smiles.

Remove all doubts and lies.

Keep a happy demeanor.

Light up your smiles with splendor.

Kiss the air with feelings,

never ever concealing.

The joy you are revealing

is love and its true meaning.

Love with a heart that's loving,

genuinely in the way you're giving,

reaching out to all around you

with compassion and understanding too.

Keep a smile upon your face.

Let all know and feel your grace.

Make your joyful presence known

to all that share your happy home.

Fill your heart with music and song.

Invite all to come along,

like a joyous caravan,

spreading joy to all you can.

Wrap your pleasures around you tight.

Enjoy them with all your might.

Take time out to share

with joyful love and care.

190. Looking through This Window of the World

Looking through this window of the world,

obscured by shadows of confusion,

through a screen of darkness,

disgusted with dreams and illusions.

Reality is colored in doubts,

while dreams are lacking in substance.

So much is unknown and disguised,

clothed in its decadence,

blackened and not recognizable,

a blanket of lies and cover-ups.

While searching for understanding

and finding only what's corrupt,

floating in a cloud of deception,

covered by promises and lies.

Nothing to expose the clutter,

in a designed system of spies.

What's wrapped in the conspiracy

and covered in blind illusions,

devious and undermining,

without hope or solutions.

Acceptance with no defiance

can only mean defeat.

Without a plan or action,

we bow down to the evil elite.

191. The View from the Hilltop

The view from the hilltop

that stretches in the vast skies.

A beautifully decorated sight,

where the butterflies and eagles fly.

As a gentle breeze brushes the trees,

the colors of the blossoms spike,

pleasant and intoxicating,

in a majestic expanding sight.

Reaching out to touch the scene—

the sight and sound that music makes—

the beauty transforms the space

to pleasures felt as life awakes.

Oh, how beautiful is the morning sun,

lighting up the day as it glows,

peeking out from every crevice,

brilliant in its formation of rainbows.

As the sun walked across the sky,

the shadows darted in and out,

forming objects of delight,

here and there and all about.

The fragrance so sweet and pungent

leaves a lingering presence,

just to remind us all,

there is a place on earth like heaven.

As the golden sun is setting

and the horizon disappearing,

the land seems to kiss the sky,

with its beauty never ending.

The night sky with its abundant stars

sets a pattern of a beautiful setting.

The cool, soft light is soothing

at the close of the day's ending.

+ + +

192. The Mist and the Fog

The mist and the fog

covered the woodsmen's logs

as they lay there scattered

on the moistened sod.

This gloomy sight with its destruction,

piled high amongst the stumps,

displayed a sight of death.

A sight seen at dumps.

The woodsmen had gathered

in celebration, with laughter.

This project had ended.

No remorse for the slaughter.

Work is done—a new land cleared.

A location for a new building.

The trees have died at a cost.

The forest is left there, dying.

Progress disguised as modernization

is so ambiguous.

Destroying to justify an action

is definitely dubious.

Move aside for progress, they say.

Let nothing stand in the way.

Some would find an answer;

others are left to pray.

+ + +

193. I Walked the Streets at Night

I walked the streets at night—

all night with tired feet.

I would see strange things

in people that I meet.

Sometimes surrounded by beauty—

the cool and intoxicating air,

romantic with a bit of suspense,

with the moonlight everywhere.

The night is full of evil;

the darkness sets a mood.

Looking for some answers,

not knowing you are the fool.

Shadows popping in and out.

I follow blindly, expecting

to find some kind of solution

to a mystery I was inventing.

No good comes from wandering at night.

Often only the dark side shows itself,

wrapped up in a neat package,

and presented as a doubtful self.

At night your view is dimmed.

Things you think you see are not there.

You imagination is a runaway train,

numbed by your own inner fear.

Sleep is not a factor.

Daytime will solve that need.

This need and fixation for a night life

is the illusion that it feeds.

+ + +

194. Are We Afraid to Go Along

Are we afraid to go along

like a fearless bear,

hiding from ourselves, showing no fear?

Brave and thoughtful men die every day

while the cowards hide away in play.

Most of us are cowards.

Lying in the grass,

we hide in the darkness,

waiting for the trouble to pass.

Heroes are the few so brave.

They are frontline in a flash,

taking to the battlefield.

Never would they crash.

Accepting the abuses

is a shameless way to live.

Turning the other cheek

is the wrong impression we give.

Two wrongs do not make a right

in a discussion or a fight.

To be truthful to anyone else,

we must first be truthful to ourselves.

The devil is a demon

without a care at all.

The only thought he's having

is to see how many will fall.

There is no screen to hide behind,

or any hole to crawl inside.

Walk a proud line and lift your head high.

Never let the pride in you die.

195. Moonlight and Sunsets

Moonlight and sunsets

brighten up our lives.

Romance and sunrises

paint our faces with smiles.

Friends and love ones around us

make a difference in this world.

The joys and happiness they bring

would never ever get old.

Everything around us,

and the beauty that it shares,

lifts our hearts and spirits.

It's there for all who care.

Dance and song feed our very soul.

Flowers, butterflies and bees,

making the honey sweet,

given to all for free.

Laughter sets the mood

for all around to see.

The joys that are in us

shine bright like sunny seas.

Holding hands and sharing

these bounties here on land,

mixed with understanding,

left here for woman and man.

196. When Roses Are in Bloom

When roses are in bloom,

listening to your favorite tune,

the mood is set for the day.

Let my music play.

The air is full of wonders

as you sit and ponder.

What would the day bring

while the birds sing?

The wind is blowing silently

from the hills to the valley.

The morning shadows melting,

like winter into spring.

A lazy day full of nothing,

riding on a wing.

No worries to pull you down,

just the wind and your song.

Tomorrow is another day,

yet so far away.

Sunset, moonlight and dawn

would morph into the morn.

Let the rain fall down

like music of a song.

Watch the water splatter around

like a merry-go-round.

197. Give Thanks and Praise

Give thanks and praise

to God each day.

Bow your head down;

be truthful when you pray.

Don't make believe

or take things for granted.

God knows all

and who's pretending.

Speak to God

what's on your mind.

You will get an answer;

be patient and you'll find.

Thank God for what is given,

seen or not seen.

Don't be blinded

with a mind unclean.

Days would come and days would go.

Rain may fall or even snow.

Your prayers will be answered,

and then you'll know.

Believe with true faith;

you'll not be disappointed.

God works in mysterious ways,

and your head will be anointed.

198. Sad Eyes Cry from the Inside

Sad eyes cry from the inside

Drops of tears do subside

Seeking not for sympathy

From a friend or enemy

Uncertain future without plans

Unknown circumstances stand

Not knowing where to turn

Left alone with worried concerns

Hopeless and left in isolation

Looking for any solution

Doubts that full your worry head

Seeking truthful answers instead

How to make a good decision

Met with uncertain conclusions

Never knowing what the outcome

Or where the fix may come from

Looking above for guidance

Waiting for change in silence

Not knowing what tomorrow brings

Or how the pendulum swings

Trust in God with unbridled faith

Expectations and hope he creates

The darkness will not forever dominate

However long one must wait

199. An Unattainable Desire

An unattainable desire,

like an unquenchable fire.

Wanting what cannot be attained

or possibly acquired.

Reaching out without success.

A determined fate amiss.

Trying to achieve a goal

with an effort so bold.

Making efforts to connect

with awkward determination.

Finding ways to articulate,

mixed with frustration.

What appears to be out of reach

is not invisible, it seems.

Without persistence,

hope is lost in a dream.

Rejection can leave a scar,

deep and unrepairable.

To achieve what you desire

can always be attainable.

Fill a bucket with all your desires

and watch them disappear.

Choose one you truly desire

and pursue without fear.

200. It Will Take a Prodigious Effort

It will take a prodigious effort

to find utopia,

a journey that may take

forever.

To find a paradise would require

a determination,

a persistent effort

with undying dedication.

A perfect place to discover,

to find peace covered in mystery.

The search never ending,

a start of a new history.

Where is it hiding?

Is it worth finding?

Look far and wide.

But first look inside.

Is there such a dreamland,

a place free of misfortunes and crimes?

Or is it an illusion

we will never find?

A perfect place,

a perfect space—

Where can it be

if not in the heart of me?

+ + +

201. And Just the Two

And just the two

made a hidden rendezvous.

Not by chance.

A hidden romance.

The night was dark,

without a spark.

The time was set,

with no regrets.

No one should know—

not friends or foe.

A plan was made.

They were not afraid.

It was just the two.

No one knew.

In the dark of night,

they planned their flight.

With feelings strong,

what could be wrong?

A moment of passion

without condition.

A kiss or two,

and promises too.

No other eyes had seen

this beautiful scene.

The night had ended.

No one offered

plans for a future,

about a walk down the altar.

They planned to elope

with heighten hope.

What could go wrong

with a love so strong?

+ + +

202. Memories Can Be Forever

Memories can be forever.

They stay around if you let them.

Some you learn from, some you dismiss.

Some bring pleasures, some you resist.

Memories are not made by themselves.

They are your very own creations.

They will come back to you

when you least expect them to.

Memories are a great possession,

sometimes impossible to dismiss.

Some would bring you laughter—

others, total disaster.

Hold on to your memories.

They are precious;

they can bring a smile to your face

that time cannot erase.

As you travel through life's roads,

the memories you create

will be your greatest gift.

They will give your spirit a lift.

+ + +

203. Is It What You See?

Is it what you see,

what you want it to be?

Or is it unreal

when revealed?

Like a painting on the wall,

seen by one and all,

appears to be so perfect,

yet hides all its defects.

On an empty canvas space,

the artist paints a face.

The likes of what he knows

with each stroke of his brush flow.

The model in his mind

is left for you to find.

An image you once knew

is sometimes led askew.

The picture that you see,

full of life and gaiety,

is the artist's point of view,

left for interpretation too.

What's real is seldom seen

if hidden in a dream.

Awake to see what's real,

the real from the unreal.

+ + +

204. There Are Dreams I Remember

There are dreams I remember

from when I was a youngster:

what I wanted to see

and what I wanted to be.

Visiting lands far away from home

with no fear of how far I roamed—

through forest and trickling streams,

climbing high mountains in my dreams,

meeting exotic people far and wide,

safe in my dreams I would hide.

I would close my eyes and roam

as I mingle in the natives' homes.

The beautiful places I would go,

bathed in sunshine or snow.

The vast oceans, rivers and moats,

I would sail in my imaginary boat.

Like a bird I would soar above the sky,

viewing the desert with an eagle's eyes.

Moving from place to place,

acquiring knowledge with haste.

Dreams can become reality;

in my imagination I can see.

Places, people and things of value

can only be real with me and you.

205. She Was a Troubled Soul

She was a troubled soul,

not so brave and not so bold,

caught in a vicious cycle,

unable to remove the obstacles.

Her life was in a downward spiral.

She had so many rivals.

She danced alone to the drumbeat

in the crowded streets.

She was no entertainer;

those she knew had failed her.

Left alone to survive,

she smiled with tearful eyes.

It was a hard way to go on living,

with her dancing and her singing.

But no choice was given

if she needed to keep on living.

Her mistakes and regrets

made her never forget.

This road she had taken

was hopeless and forsaken.

There were so many reasons,

and it was not very easy.

She took a lover,

belonging to another.

He never loved her—

the husband of her sister.

A bond was destroyed

for a moment of joy.

It is such a sad story—

no love no glory.

Her telling of those lies

left her in exile.

+ + +

206. Oh, Sleep, Where Can You Be?

Oh, sleep, where can you be?

Why have you abandoned me?

Forsaken in this twilight hour

like a prisoner in an unknown tower.

Drifting into a frozen zone.

Slipping into the unknown.

Sleep will not enter

while my mind is full of wonder.

Up all night, staring at the ceiling,

not understanding the meaning.

Trying hard to fall asleep,

losing count while counting sheep.

The night slowly turns into morning.

Not one moment of sleeping.

Sleep—oh, sleep—where have you gone,

hiding where you can't be found?

Looking for the sandman's blessings,

wondering if it's sleep he's giving.

Wide awake till the morning dawning.

Waiting for sleep but no sleep coming.

+ + +

207. The Past Is Gone Forever

The past is gone forever.

Mistakes you can change.

Tomorrow is a new chapter

to put a picture in the right frame.

Should have gone left.

Maybe even right.

The choice you made then

was never a clear sight.

What is done

cannot be undone.

The future is a mystery

for you and everyone.

Some would bite the bullet.

Others would make a change.

Not all would work out as planned.

Some remain the same.

Living with the mistakes

is sometimes hard to do.

Making constructive changes

is only for the few.

A lifetime is not forever,

to settle or compromise.

The brave would take a different path

and follow the bold and wise.

208. Open Your Heart to All

Open your heart to all.

Listen to God's call.

With an open mind,

generosity you'll find.

Can you see your brother in need

and not respond or heed?

Cast a blind eye to his folly

without showing any apathy?

Fortunes come and go,

like water in a river flow,

without fear of retribution,

giving to ease a situation.

A rich man believes in accumulating.

A wise man gets joy in giving.

Helping a fellow human being—

to all an act of love is seen.

When your cup is full of gold,

sharing with an unfortunate soul

can only bring gratification

to you and one of God's creation.

What you acquire and gather,

you would leave as fodder.

We take nothing when we expire.

Don't burn your riches on a funeral pyre.

209. How Long Will This Memory Last?

How long will this memory last,

awakened by a betrayal from my past?

An image of you comes back to me.

I tried so hard to forget and be free.

Her love, she said, was for only me,

but it was illusion, not reality.

I close my eyes, but still I see.

The love I lost would never be.

So long ago in another time,

I lost your love that was never mine.

You loved another I did not know.

I was the one that had to go.

I moved on, trying to forget that,

but your memory keep pulling me back.

Like a fool I want to keep it alive,

hoping that spark could still survive.

A heart that's broken is hard to mend.

I try to forget and let it end.

Lost in a love as it was before,

even a lifetime could not restore.

+ + +

210. I Never Loved Another

I never loved another

the way I love you.

I wanted you to know

I will never make you blue.

The look of your face

is not all that attracted me.

Your charm and grace

are the beauty that I see.

That special feeling

I get when I hold your hand

lights up my inside

brighter than a fairy's wand.

One kiss from you

puts me in a trance.

My heart is so happy,

all I want to do is dance.

Someone like you

is very hard to find.

I am so thankful

that you're really mine.

+ + +

211. This Story Is Very Old

This story is very old

but must be told—

a story of a mother

and her lovely daughter.

In a far-off land,

at the edge of the desert sand,

there lived a girl

in a troubled world.

She fell for a man

not of her clan.

He once saved her life

and wanted her to be his wife.

He was a man very well known,

with lots of wealth and gold.

Her mother thought he was too old

to marry her daughter young and bold.

He was three time her age,

and she would become his slave.

He had many slaves.

He was ruthless and brave.

He was nearing his end,

and her daughter would be sent

to be put to death as his bride

whenever he died.

The mother would decide:

her daughter she would hide.

So she locked away the girl

to save her life I am told.

212. Compassion or Kindness

Compassion or Kindness.

Joy or happiness.

Charity or sharing.

Concern or worrying.

Is white the color of knowledge?

Is red the color of pain?

Is age a state of mind?

Is black the paint of the insane?

Looking with eyes that doesn't see.

Seeing only what's visible to see.

A perception that's faulted,

while trying to escape the inevitability.

A vail covers the truth

that black thoughts try to hide.

A true light can reveal its source

or show what's hidden inside.

Dark shadows conceal

what is real,

while covering it with pleasantries

so it cannot be revealed.

Truth, kindness and compassion

can never be compromised

or driven underground

by hidden agendas and lies.

+ + +

213. A Dagger Has Two Sharp Sides

A dagger has two sharp sides.

An evil man has two faces of lies.

The constant reaching for the prize,

not caring who loses or cries.

The ego that feed the greed,

and the evil web it weaves.

No regard for fellow man.

Never lifting a helping hand.

A selfish way of life instead.

Only the greedy would be fed.

There is no limit to this greed,

ignoring the innocent as they bleed.

How much is needed to be satisfied?

There is no shame, compassion or pride.

To gather more than one can need

is the objective of those with greed.

Greed has no limit and no end.

Greed has no honor and no friend.

What little nest one possesses

is quickly lost to greediness.

The greedy never truthfully get wealthy;

they take from others so easily.

They find some other unscrupulous way

to take from others anyway.

214. What's in the Past Must Stay in the Past

What's in the past must stay in the past.

It only becomes good memories if it lasts.

A wish is a hope that never materializes.

Trying to change the past is living a lie.

Memories brings a smile to your face,

reliving great times and space,

thinking of the many things you did,

remembering when you were just a kid.

The moonlight on a summer night.

Your first kiss as you held her tight.

Remembering all those things and more:

how outdoors you slept on the floor.

Remembering the good and the bad,

also the scary and the sad.

The way we talked all through night

and stayed up till morning light.

So many things to remember still,

you never could get your fill.

People and places you thought about

linger in your memory throughout.

Rest your thoughts on memories at night.

They can take you on a pleasant flight.

Your dreams would brighten them up,

and good memories would never stop.

215. Memories come back one by one

Memories come back one by one

of when we had so much fun.

I try to remember only some,

the happy not the sad ones.

The nights are full of thoughts—

the beauty that she brought,

the sadness of her eyes

whenever she would cry.

I sit and think of her some days

and the funny things she'll say.

They always bring back the blues

to soothe this old and lonely fool.

The memories of her face and eyes

leave tracks of tears as I cry.

The way her heart was so kind,

and her promises so divine.

Memories are like anchors in the sand,

left there to give a helping hand.

Something to hold onto

whenever I get melancholy and blue.

+ + +

216. Look in the Mirror: All You See Is You

Look in the mirror: All you see is you.

What you are, what you've become.

A bright, shining star

or a useless bum.

A reflection of yourself

is sometimes hard to take.

It is truly real,

but you wish it was a fake.

Turn the mirror around,

but the image does not disappear.

It still exists,

the very image you fear.

Wipe your face, wipe the mirror,

the reflection remains the same.

Even with a deceptive smile,

the mirror is not to be blamed.

Every one you meet

sees you as your mirrors do.

What is true or false,

and what is really you.

Break the mirror into a thousand pieces;

it can never change the true you.

All the makeup and disguise you use,

you remain you whatever you do.

+ + +

217. Come with Me

Come with me.

We'll fly to another galaxy.

Traveling on clouds,

just joyful and carefree.

Soaring with the wind.

Traveling to another sphere,

leaving a troubled world,

floating in open air.

Making believe.

Engulfed in our imagination,

we will be warmed by the sun.

Making new creations.

The moon and the sky

will be our playground.

We will dance with angels,

while singing love songs.

We will go planet hopping,

with a visit to the moon.

When asked when we'll be back,

we'll answer, "Not too soon."

Leaving the stars behind,

we'll find our way,

flying all around

into the Milky Way.

+ + +

218. What Has Love Done for You?

What has love done for you?

Is it something from the past?

Why do you keep it at arms' length?

Are you afraid of a broken heart?

A heart cannot be broken

when there is joy felt.

A moment of happiness

is greater than your wealth.

A deep and special moment,

a journey to a kiss.

A chance you must take

to achieve a feeling of bliss.

Love is a selfish feeling,

not necessarily shared by two.

It matters not

if love is felt by who.

Giving love or getting love—

it all depends on you.

True love that is shared

is only by the few.

To love and be loved

can be the greatest joy.

You'll be the loser

if you never loved at all.

Love is not your enemy.

It can be such a friend

if you let it.

It will never end.

Love is a miracle.

If you let it grow,

it can last forever.

You may never know.

You must not let love pass

by pretending you don't care.

Sometimes love can blossom

if you throw away your fear.

Do not lock love out,

afraid to be smitten.

Love is very powerful

once you're bitten.

+ + +

219. She Said She Lost Her Love

She said she lost her love

and would like to find another.

Would she consider me?

I wondered.

I would not take advantage

of the situation.

But I think

we'll make a good union.

What would she think of it?

Or was ours just a friendship?

I sure would like to suggest

we both start afresh.

At our first meeting,

there was an attraction.

But I am so afraid

of rejection.

I know we'll be good for each other.

If she would only consider

a new start to the future,

together forever and ever.

I will wait for her answer,

even if it's forever.

Waiting, anticipating,

a new love beginning.

+ + +

220. You Can't Turn Back Time

You can't turn back time,

except in dreams

or memories

or songs that rhyme.

Time waits for no man,

no matter how fast he ran.

Capture time and put in a bottle—

see if you can.

Like a spoken word

or a croaking toad,

an arrow that's left the bow,

it will never come back.

Neither a rooster's crow.

Waiting for time to repeat itself,

it will pass you in a flash.

If you don't use it,

it will be impossible to catch.

Hold onto time and think it will stay,

as the night changes into day,

like the waves in the ocean

continue breaking toward the bay.

Time is of the essence.

It is also immortal, and yet,

when you've used up all your time,

there is no more time left.

+ + +

221. Melodious and Mellow as a Cello

Melodious and mellow as a cello,

sounds from a distant radio.

The fragrance of your presence—

your substance and your essence—

thrills me so.

Like the music of the wind,

the golden voice as you sing.

A nightingale cannot compare,

while I delight in a love affair.

I am in a trance.

An echo in the distance—

a wonderful performance—

simple yet captivating.

Heartfelt and warming,

soothing my mind.

A touch and an explosion.

A feeling of elation,

riding on clouds of joys.

Rejoicing in a stupendous ploy,

I surrender.

Wrapped in a blanket of calm

made of soft cotton crocheted yarn.

In a relaxed frame of mind,

sipping on a sparkling wine,

I sit and smile.

A magical night in summer,

together with your lover,

under the starlit sky as cover.

Listening with delightful wonder,

I fall asleep.

222. I Can Hear the Robins Sing

I can hear the robins sing.

It must be spring.

I hear music in the distance

prompting lovers to dance.

On this wonderful evening,

spring blossoms are blooming.

Love is in the air,

and our world is without care.

My view from the window

reveals your shadow.

A silhouette of your beauty

is all that I can see.

Like a magical spring day,

we dance and sway.

The rhythm is smooth and slow;

the music plays sweet and low.

We dance all night

under the golden moonlight.

I whisper in your ear,

"I am so glad you're here."

Summers are so warm and clear.

The winter's cold will disappear.

Autumn is full of rain,

but spring is here again.

+ + +

223. Your Fragrance and Elegance

Your fragrance and elegance.

Your thoughts and your eloquence.

Your presence brightens the hour

like the radiant scent of a flower.

Your eyes are like a diamond's glitters,

shining bright as it quivers.

Your smile and your radiance

set the tone of your brilliance.

With your head held high,

the pride you carry is sublime.

You are a pillar standing strong

that all are honored to be around.

A mysterious light sets you aglow

to everyone it shows.

A beacon you have become

to me and to everyone.

Your friendship I would treasure,

something I will have forever.

Your trust and your confidence

would always give me guidance.

When you've found a true friend,

that friendship never ends.

It weathers every storm,

and it defines all the norms.

+ + +

224. A Piece of the Pie

A piece of the pie

before you die.

Is it in sight,

or a dreamer's plight?

Restricted by your ancestors

or viewed by other factors.

With or without college,

is equality based on knowledge?

You are not wrong; it's your right

to not have to fight for equal rights,

based on exploitation,

or even by segregation.

Stand proud on your merit,

with a personality that fit.

All is equal in God's eyes.

Morality a victory for the wise.

A one-sided view of someone

is not the practice of everyone.

Togetherness is a mighty force,

a strength that can stay the course.

Wisdom is not shared by all.

Some would rise, and some would fall.

All should have an equal chance

to fail or deservingly advance.

Color stigma or a different faith—

neither carries any weight.

Love for your fellow man

would make a world we all understand.

225. Old Habits Keep Coming Back

Old habits keep coming back,

like a monkey on your back.

Old habits are here to stay.

They never really go away.

For all you try to forget,

bad habits keep coming back.

You try to think of something new,

but old habits stay with you.

Try as you may to let old habits be,

they never let you be free.

Old habits you can't control

stay with you as you get old.

You take old habits wherever you go.

You try to hide them, but still they show.

Old habits are hard to break.

They seldom let new habits take their place.

Old habits you can't destroy

stay with you like precious toys.

Old habits seldom change.

If you try, they change back again.

Old habits possess a venom of regrets,

sometimes hard to forget.

Old habits, you will see,

linger in your darkest memory.

Old habits you will try to shake

lie dormant but will soon awake.

Old habits will never go away.

They will stay with you until you are gray.

Old habits are like precious stones:

they never leave you alone.

They make up your mind for you,

no matter what you say or do.

Old habits are embedded in you,

like a comfortable broken-in shoe.

Some old habits can save the day,

but most old habits you can throw away.

+ + +

226. I Thought of an Old Friend Today

I thought of an old friend today

and wondered what he would say.

How we used to spend the day,

and the games we used to play.

We would take a trip to Mars,

riding on some twinkling stars.

We had breakfast on the moon

while we sang our favorite tune.

I would tell him of my eloquence

and lie about my girlfriends.

He would listen to me tentatively,

and then he'd say, supposedly.

We would ride high to the top,

drinking beer from the same cup.

We would sit and talk about everything that don't amount

to nothing.

Sometimes we would play our guitars,

pretending we were rock stars.

We were such a carefree pair,

without a worry or a care.

We invited all that we could

to join us in the hood.

We would dance and sing

and did most everything.

Those days were precious to us.

We never made a fuss.

We parted ways one dreadful day,

but the memories made are here to stay.

+ + +

227. The Path to a True Heart

The path to a true heart

was always there from the start.

Never recognizing it was so,

only a fool would not know.

No tears before the laughter.

The hatred for your brother

never appears to go away.

Deceptive games you want to play.

To look beyond the hate,

believing with true faith.

Forgiveness is an easy deed,

to forget the selfish greed.

Life is a precious gift you possess.

In time it's all you have left.

Use it wisely; it's the only one you get.

Live it well without regrets.

Everyone feels their burden is great,

though all can endure the weight.

Life unfolds without disguise.

You will see with your own eyes.

The need to grab what's not yours—

a desire to own all the toys—

will get you quicker to the grave,

never accumulating all you crave.

A lesson to learn from all of this:

be fair to all who exist.

Forgive and treat all the same.

Life is not an egotistical game.

228. In My Dream I Can Build a Wall

In my dream I can build a wall

around myself,

isolated from everyone else.

I can now create this vast estate—

build castles with golden gates.

I will possess untold riches,

surrounded by beautiful palaces.

I will not have a golden crown.

Nor would I wear a king's gown.

In my dream I can go to extremes,

so I would make you my queen.

You would be my perfect wife,

and we would have a happy life.

We would go on magical carpet rides,

traveling the world to see the sights.

We would lunch on the highest mountains

and have dinner by our favorite fountains.

All would be at our feet.

We'll be kind to all we meet.

On special days we'll devise a plan

to share the fortunes of all the land.

But life is not a dream; it's real.

Neither is it surreal.

With your feet firmly on the ground,

reality is real, and it's all around.

+ + +

229. A Dubious Act of Deception

A dubious act of deception

Is dangerous as a poisonous serpent.

Hidden in the proverbial grass,

Ambiguous and without class,

Prying on the innocent to lend,

Disguised as a trusted friend.

Beware of silver-tongued greed.

The only aim is to deceive.

Taking from the trusting one,

Unaware of the devious con.

Promises of brighter days ahead

With hidden agendas instead.

A wonderful picture painted at best.

A guarantee of total success.

Figures to attract the amateur

While concealing a negative failure.

The venom so skillfully disguised

Is only recognized by the wise.

Look beneath each buried stone

Before you commit to all your own.

+ + +

230. Compassion and empathy

Compassion and empathy

Are excellent qualities.

A thought of your fellow man

Is noble and grand.

A kind act of understanding

Can be so rewarding.

A pleasant thought for others

Like helping your sisters and brothers.

A thoughtful gesture toward someone

Can be rewarding and lots of fun,

With not a hint of personal gain,

Just the pure joy without the fame.

Giving to others with generosity

Is clearly a feeling of empathy.

To give openly without rewards

Is a quality one can clearly afford.

Share with love and sympathy

So all can plainly see.

An act of kindness is a Godly act.

Rewards most certainly will come back

+ + +

231. It's Your Memories That Held Me Captive

It's your memories that held me captive,

remembering the past.

When we were young, so long ago,

we never thought love would last.

A spark that ignited—

a feeling I have missed—

thinking of those days,

I would reminisce.

Youthful energy we possessed.

No thought of togetherness.

The thrill of that first kiss—

a life together we missed.

Faith has a way

of making things come through.

A joyous reunion,

just for me and you.

Now in our twilight years,

a dream is fulfilled.

Side by side once again—

it must be God's will.

HISTORIES OF THE UNEXPECTED
The Vikings

Sam Willis & James Daybell

Atlantic Books
London

First published in Great Britain in 2019 by Atlantic Books,
an imprint of Atlantic Books Ltd.

1 2 3 4 5 6 7 8 9

A CIP catalogue record for this book is available from
the British Library.

Hardback ISBN: 978-1-78649-771-0
E-book ISBN: 978-1-78649-772-7

Printed and bound by CPI Group (UK) Ltd, Croydon, CR0 4YY

Atlantic Books
An Imprint of Atlantic Books Ltd
Ormond House
26–27 Boswell Street
London
WC1N 3JZ

www.atlantic-books.co.uk

For

Kate	*Felix*
&	*&*
Alice	*Bea*

CONTENTS

Everything

HAS A *history* EVEN THE MOST unexpected OF SUBJECTS…

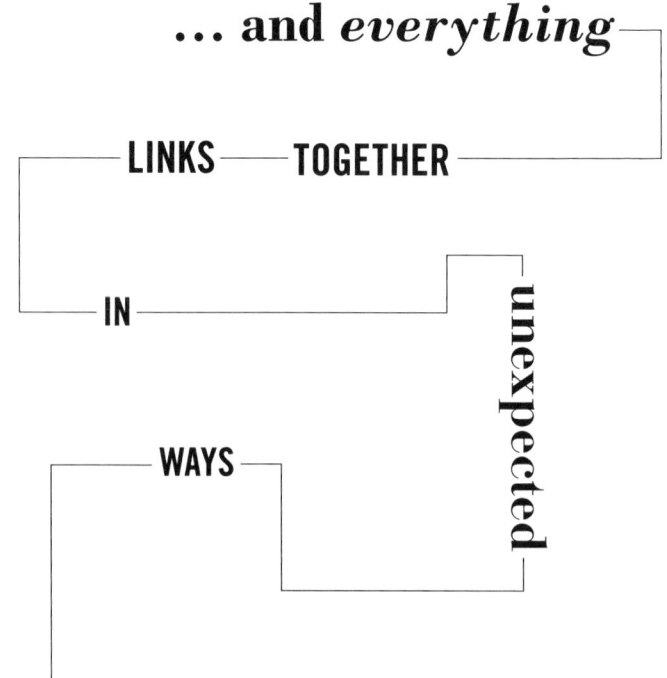

… and *everything* LINKS TOGETHER IN unexpected WAYS

A PERSONAL NOTE

At Histories of the Unexpected, we believe that everything has a history – even the most unexpected of subjects – and that everything links together in unexpected ways.

We believe that the itch, crawling, clouds, lightning, zombies and zebras and holes and perfume and rubbish and mustard – each has a fascinating history of its own.

In this book we take this approach into the Viking world. You will find out how the history of graffiti is all to do with Viking travel; how the history of teeth is connected to Viking identity; and how the history of doors is all about the Viking dead.

To explore and enjoy subjects in this way will change not only how you think about the past, but also the present. It is enormously rewarding, and we encourage you all to join in! Find us online at www.historiesoftheunexpected.com and on Twitter @ UnexpectedPod – and do please get in touch.

ACKNOWLEDGEMENTS

All of our Histories of the Unexpected books are about sharing great research and new approaches to history. Our first acknowledgement, therefore, must go to all of those brilliant historians – professional and amateur – who are writing today and who are changing the way that we think about the past. You are all doing a fabulous job, and one which often goes unremarked and unrewarded. Thank you for your time, effort, energy and insight. We could not have written this book without you.

Since this book is intended for a wide and general audience, we have chosen not to publish with extensive footnotes. We acknowledge our indebtedness to fellow historians in the Selected Further Reading section at the end of the book, which is also intended as a spur to further research for our readers.

We would like to thank the many colleagues and friends who have generously offered ideas, guidance, support and sustenance, intellectual and otherwise: Anthony Caleshu, Lee Jane Giles, Dan Maudlin, Svante Norrhem, the Lord John Russell, Christopher Tyerman, Teva Vidal, Matthew Delvaux, Vibeke Bischoff, Line Bregnøi, Eva Thäte, Mads Christien Christensen, Josefine Frank Bican, Morten Ravn; and among the twitterati, @HunterSJones, @RedLunaPixie, @KittNoir and @Kazza2014.

Collective thanks are also due to Dan Snow, Natt Tapley, James Carson, Tom Clifford and the fabulous History Hit team for all their support and encouragement, as well as to Will Atkinson, James Nightingale, Kate Straker, Jamie Forrest and everyone at Atlantic Books.

We would also like to thank everyone (and there are hundreds of thousands of you) who has listened to the podcast or come to see one of our live events and been so charming and enthusiastic.

Most of all, however, we would like to thank our families, young and old, for everything they have done and continue to do, to cope with – *of all things* – a historian in their lives.

But we have created this book for you.

Sam and James

Isca – Escanceaster – Exeter
The Feast of St Benedict – 8-Dhū al-Qaʻdah 1440 – I.VII.MMXIX – 11 July 2019

THE VIKINGS:
AN INTRODUCTION

A Viking helm found in Gjermundbu, Norway, tenth century. It has been
scarred from a sword blow and punctured by an arrow

WHO WERE THEY?

The term 'Viking' has changed meaning over time. Originally it meant 'robbers' and was used to describe coastal raiders, but more recently it has come to denote a people who lived in Scandinavia but who also spread out across the majority of northern Europe between c.700 and c.1400. It has even been used to name the entire chronological period in which this happened: the Viking Age.

It is not clear whether the word originated in Scandinavia, and it was not widely used at the time. It appears only four times before 1066 in the most comprehensive history of the period – the *Anglo-Saxon Chronicle* – and only in its native English forms of *wícenga* or *wícinga*. It was not used in other countries who suffered raids, where the Vikings' religious beliefs led to them being dismissed as 'pagans' or 'heathens'. In Ireland they were the *Gaill*, simply meaning 'foreigners'; elsewhere they were referred to by their geographical origin: Norsemen from the north, or Danes from the south.

Scandinavians thought of themselves as coming from particular regions, such as Jutland in the south or Hordaland in the west. In fact, some linguists argue that the word 'Viking' originates from *vík*, the name for a wick – or bay – and is thought to refer to a very specific area of south-east Norway around the Oslo Fjord and inland coastal region.

Setting this complexity aside, these people spoke the same language – Old Norse – and they shared many aspects of a vibrant, complex and common culture. What we *can* say, therefore, is that the Vikings were a unique and distinctive people who originated in Scandinavia but who sent out men and women far beyond its boundaries – to violently rob, extort and conquer, but also to peacefully trade, settle and farm.

Vikings were far more than violent marauders. They were warriors, sailors, inventors, mystics, merchants, farmers, fishermen, explorers, ambassadors, diplomats, craftsmen, musicians, poets, wives, mothers, husbands, fathers and children. They changed the world that they lived in, and they shaped the world as we know it today.

THE VIKING AGE

The concept of the 'Viking Age' is no less straightforward, and historians disagree about when it began and ended. For those living around the time of the Viking Age, it depended entirely on where you lived: indeed, it is exactly this question which most powerfully elicits the scope of the Viking achievement.

Both historical and archaeological evidence shows that Scandinavians had achieved a certain level of state formation and outward expansion by the early years of the eighth century, but it was not until the 790s that their impact was truly felt – with the start of their violent raids.

In the British Isles, raiding activities began with an attack on the holy site and monastery of Lindisfarne in Northumbria in 793, followed by one on the monastery on the Scottish island of Iona in 794 and several attacks on Irish monasteries in 795. The raids continued and intensified. The year 841 saw a permanent Viking camp in Dublin, which subsequently became a major Viking trading centre. They also headed south in this period, reaching Lisbon and Seville in the 840s. Throughout the 850s attacks were launched into Francia (modern-day France) and Spain. They also travelled east, attacking Constantinople in 860 and settling in Novgorod, in what is now Russia, in 862. Thereafter, they raided as far as the Black and Caspian seas and even Baghdad. From the late 870s, Vikings settled in England and ruled large parts of the country in the north and east; they founded colonies on the Isle of Man, the Northern and Western Isles, and they settled Iceland. In the 980s they settled Greenland and made voyages west to what is now Newfoundland, which the Vikings knew as Vinland, around 1000.

The 'end' of the Viking Age also depended on where you were. It has traditionally been seen in England as 1066, with the death at the Battle of Stamford Bridge of the Norwegian king Harald Hardrada, and the subsequent invasion of England by William, Duke of Normandy. However, William himself – as well as many of his nobles, who subsequently ruled vast tracts of England – was of direct Viking descent, the great-great-great grandson of Rollo, the Viking who seized Rouen in 876 and became the first ruler of Normandy. William even invaded in 'Viking' ships.

Thus the Norman conquest of England in 1066 was as much 'Viking' as it was 'French'. At this time and after, Scandinavians were still very much present in Scotland, Ireland and the Isle of Man, and Viking culture continued in Iceland and Greenland – and, of course, the Scandinavian homelands themselves – well into the fifteenth century.

Such a massive geographical area and lengthy period of time – which necessitates drawing on markedly diverse source materials from the eighth to fourteenth centuries – present historians with significant problems of interpretation: 'Vikings' and the 'Viking Age' are slippery customers indeed.

THE EVIDENCE

A remarkably broad range of evidence survives – literary and visual, archaeological and scientific – that sheds light on Vikings and Viking activity. And in spite of the gaps that necessarily remain in the study of a diverse society well over 1,200 years old, an imaginative approach that incorporates all forms of this evidence has allowed historians and archaeologists to reconstruct many aspects of Viking society and culture.

Frustratingly, very few written sources were actually produced by the Vikings themselves. The contemporary documents that do survive – letters, legal codes, chronicles, and histories such as the anonymous *Anglo-Saxon Chronicle* and Gregory of Tours's *History of the Franks* – were produced by literate people (often churchmen) who came into contact with the Scandinavians and who viewed them as dangerous strangers.

One of the finest examples of such documents is also one of the first. In 793, the scholar and clergyman Alcuin of York wrote to King Æthelred of Northumbria, describing the raid on Lindisfarne:

> Lo, it is nearly 350 years that we and our fathers have inhabited this most lovely land, and never before has such terror appeared in Britain as we have now suffered from a pagan race, nor was it thought that such an inroad from the sea could be made. Behold, the church of St Cuthbert spattered with the blood of the priests of God, despoiled of all its ornaments; a place more venerable than all in Britain is given as a prey to pagan peoples.

The *Anglo-Saxon Chronicle* reported similarly that 'the ravaging of wretched heathen men' which 'destroyed God's church at Lindisfarne' was preceded by 'foreboding omens', including famine, whirlwinds, lightning and 'fiery dragons... seen flying in the sky'. Similar themes were treated in Wulfstan's 'Sermon of the Wolf', dating from the early eleventh century, in which the Archbishop of York interpreted the recent Viking raids as God's divine punishment for a lack of English moral discipline.

Christian writers often described early Viking raids in such apocalyptic terms, focusing on the ferocity and destruction of Viking activities. This kind of source perpetuated a long-standing – but now long-defunct – myth of the men from the North being nothing more than violent pagans.

Other sources include travellers' reports, such as the eyewitness account of the Arabic diplomat Ahmad ibn Fadlan (877–960) in his *Risala*, which describes life among the tenth-century Rus or Volga Vikings, and the account of the Arab traveller Ibrahim ibn Yaqub al-Tartushi, in which he recorded his visit to the famous Viking trading centre of Hedeby in Jutland.

Another form of written source is the rich tradition of saga literature that was compiled in Iceland during the thirteenth century, long after the Viking Age in England had ended. These magnificent written works were based on stories passed down the generations as part of a centuries-old oral tradition. They echo earlier contemporary culture and practices, and are soaked with references to Viking beliefs, historical events, myths and politics – but, as they were compiled relatively late, they must be handled by the historian with care.

One type of early Viking writing that does survive is runes, which are inscribed using the Scandinavian futhark alphabet. Runic inscriptions have been found in a multitude of unexpected locations – on wood, stone and even on coins. They normally take the form of short phrases, sometimes including the name of the rune-carver and the date, and they occasionally refer to historical events.

Viking influence across northern Europe even survives in modern place names, and these are studied by historians in their own right for what they can tell us about Viking integration into the societies they invaded. In England, for example, places ending in the suffix -*by* (Grimsby), -*thorpe* (Scunthorpe) or -*toft* (Lowestoft) show evidence of Viking influence, as well as 'Grimston hybrids', which are a merging of Anglo-Saxon (such as -*ton*, meaning 'town' or 'village') and Viking (the name *Grimr*) words.

Alongside these written sources, an astonishingly rich archaeological record survives in the remains of Viking settlements, from houses, shops and feasting halls to forts, ships and camps. Burial mounds across the Viking world have blessed archaeologists with some of the most extraordinary artefacts ever excavated, and numerous hoards of buried silver have transformed our understanding of Viking economics as well as providing armies of amateur metal detectorists with the motivation to carry on their search.

SEAFARING

The Vikings were able to trade and raid across such a huge geographical area because of their expertise as sailors, which was unrivalled in the northern hemisphere. They used the sun, moon and stars to navigate in open waters, along with clues from the clouds, wind, weather, smells, sounds and even animal behaviour. When close to shore they used natural seamarks to guide them into anchorages, and built new seamarks where nature did not provide a solution. That said, navigation in this period was still very much an art form rather than a science, and the Vikings even had a specific word – *hafvilla* – meaning 'lost at sea'.

At a glance, Viking ship design was uniform; their vessels were powered by oars and a single square sail. They were open-decked and double-ended; that is to say that the ship did not have a prow or stern distinguishable by design. In reality, however, there was a vast variety of fishing boats, coastal traders, ocean-going traders, royal yachts and small warships, as well as the iconic warships of the Vikings: the large longships.

We know from experiments with recreated Viking boats that these vessels were impressively seaworthy. Their unique construction gave them a remarkable level of flexibility to absorb the force of large waves; the balanced side-rudders were ideally suited to such craft and were effective even in rough seas. The ships could achieve as much as seven knots under oar alone, and they could even make progress in the direction from which the wind was blowing by repeatedly tacking across it. Perhaps most importantly for the work Viking sailors were to undertake, the shallow draughts of these ships allowed them to sail up rivers and penetrate deep inland. The Vikings may have begun life as 'coastal raiders', but in 845 they attacked Paris – which is more than 100 miles from the sea – by sailing up the River Seine.

VIKING BELIEFS

Norse pagan belief systems were highly complex, involving mythology and the supernatural – as well as regular dialogue and exchange with their Christian counterparts.

The boundaries between the worlds of the living and the dead were fluid, as were those between humans and animals. Scandinavians worshipped a range of gods, consisting of two families: the Æsir (including Odin and Thor) and the Vanir (including Freyr and Freyja). The Norse gods were served by various supernatural beings, including giants, elves, ghosts, trolls and valkyries – female figures who scoured the battlefield choosing who lived and who died – as well as animals such as birds and wild boars.

Asgard, a large fortified floating castle, was one of the Nine Worlds and the home of the Æsir pantheon of gods. The Vanir lived in another world, Vanaheim. At the edge of their worlds were the giants, who were enemies of humans and with whom the gods constantly battled. Fearful of offending the gods, the Vikings held regular sacrificial ceremonies, and ritually deposited weapons in rivers and wetlands to appease them.

Another fundamental part of the Viking pagan belief system was the practice of sorcery and the ability to prophesy the future. Beliefs in the supernatural are manifest in the surviving material and literary sources, which throw light on the figure of the *völva*, the female 'seer' and practitioner of *seiðr*, a form of sorcery connected with predicting and shaping the future. These individuals were treated with great respect and reverence, and were a source of female power in Viking society.

Viking pagan burial practices varied, but on the whole the dead were buried fully clothed, accompanied by grave goods that they would need in their journey to the next life: weapons to fight with, games to play, money to spend, and horses, carriages and ships to help them on their way. Since people were buried with their belongings in this way, graves are an invaluable archaeological resource and tell us much about everyday life.

For many generations, Christian and pagan practices coexisted, since the Norse pantheon did not insist upon religious fidelity to one god in the way that Christianity did. But one of the most important turning points in the period was the Viking conversion to Christianity. This was a long and drawn-out process, with early missionaries operating among the Danes from the early eighth century to little effect. Renewed efforts were made during the ninth century, and high-profile royal conversions led to rulers ordering their people to convert, though more as a symbol of the monarch's power than of piety. Evidence of that popular conversion is found in grave sites, where Christian objects such as crosses started to appear in Viking graves from the eighth and ninth centuries, and burial practices began to change.

These evolving practices and beliefs make the Viking world a complex and absorbing one, where paganism jostles with Christianity, and the mythical and legendary combine with the real and historic.

SOCIETY AND CULTURE

Viking society valued courage, fellowship and generosity, and revolved around honour, family and lineage. Society was hierarchical, with landowners or magnates at the top, farmers in the middle and slaves at the bottom. This basic structure fitted an agricultural economy, but with the trading centres and towns that developed with the Viking expansion, mercantile groups jockeyed for position within the social order.

Each group knew their place, with clear divisions existing between rich and poor, free and unfree, and also between men and women. Throughout the Viking Age, men rather than women assumed public and political roles, though women achieved authority and influence within the household, or in particular roles such as that of sorceress.

Most Vikings were engaged in agriculture and lived on farms rather than in towns, and their daily lives involved tending to crops and livestock. Typically, farms were based around a longhouse, which was built of wooden planks fixed together to form bowed walls that were ship-like in appearance. The walls were lined with clay, and the roofs were sloped and made from wood or thatch. These buildings had a fire in the centre but no windows or chimneys, with nothing more than a hole in the roof for ventilation. This meant that such dwellings tended to be very smoky.

AN UNEXPECTED APPROACH

Traditionally, the Vikings have been understood in a very straightforward way, following the well-known personalities, events and themes. We think, however, that the period really comes alive if you take an *unexpected* approach to its history.

Yes, ships, raiding and trade have a fascinating history, but so too do hair, break-ins, toys, teeth, keys, birds, doors, fun, graffiti, double standards, criminal profiling, colour, saunas, silk, mischief, sorcery, goading, luck, friendship and even nicknames!

Each of these subjects is fascinating in its own right, and each also sheds new light on the traditional subjects and themes that we think we know so well.

Are you ready to unlock the Viking past? Then let's start with the history of keys...

·1·
KEYS

———

Viking Age key found in Ellesø Skovsø, Denmark

Viking keys are all about control…

Keys as a security device have a history that stretches back more than 6,000 years, and in the Viking Age the technology and complexity of locks developed significantly. During this period, we see a wide variety of sizes and designs of keys, both simple and ornamented. In Viking society, keys were a significant source of power for the people who controlled them.

THE VIKING HOUSEWIFE

In particular, the key has long been interpreted as a symbol of power for the Viking housewife. They would wear keys on chains outside their dresses as a sign of their domestic responsibility and position. Tales of married women carrying such keys are everywhere in saga literature. The poem *Rígsþula* cites 'a key-hung maiden / in goat-skin kirtle' on her way to be wed in her 'bridal linen', the key symbolizing her future married status. Legal tracts dating from the twelfth and thirteenth centuries such as *Borgartingslova* speak of a housewife's right to have the keys to the household, and archaeological evidence shows that women were buried with keys among their grave goods. For many historians, these 'female' keys represent a source of women's authority within the household: the ability to control and restrict access to domestic spaces, to secure possessions and goods.

Rígsþula

This poem, which survives in a fourteenth-century man-
uscript, tells the tale of the Norse god Ríg, the father
of mankind. He wanders the world and fathers three
classes of humans: serfs, free-born farmers and nobles.
The poem therefore contains valuable information
about the living conditions and customs of the different
social classes in the Viking world. The poem is particu-
larly enigmatic, as the conclusion has not survived the
centuries and it abruptly cuts off.

SYMBOLIC POWER

Some of the keys that have been recovered from Viking graves,
however, were actually unusable. In a way these pose historians
with a problem, but if we view the locks they opened as figura-
tive rather than literal, then we can see these keys as providing
the power to open doors from one sphere to another – perhaps
from childhood to adulthood, or from life to death.

It is no coincidence that keys have been found in numerous
Viking Age children's graves in Sweden, something archae-
ologists believe is connected to passing into other realms.
Symbolically, keys have also been associated with the power of
prediction, and this is certainly how researchers have interpreted
some of the keys found in the graves of women and children –
with the key as a way of unlocking other worlds and looking into
the future to see what changes that will bring. Viewed in this
way, women who carried keys were not simply housewives, but
carriers of knowledge, itself an important form of power.

Keys could also function as cultic or religious icons, a link
which is made clear in the poem *Þrymskviða*, where the key

is connected to the female goddess Freyja, wife of Odr. In the poem, Thor dresses up as a bride instead of Freyja in order to trick the giant Thrymr. Assuming her clothing, Thor importantly ties Freyja's 'housewife's keys' around his waist. The deception works, no doubt thanks to Thor's careful attention to detail.

Through its association with Freyja, the key is much more than a physical means of access to the household; it represents the role of Viking women as leaders, child-bearers and in the afterlife. Freyja appears in Norse mythology as ruler in the hall of Sessrúmnir in the meadow of Fólkvangr, where half of those who die in battle go. As the key-bearer, she is therefore a keeper of the dead in the afterlife. She is also a goddess of fertility, and figures in Norse mythology as a helper of women in labour. In the realm of childbirth, the key was viewed as a device to unlock women's loins, and it was also a pre-Christian symbol of female fertility and motherhood.

KEYS AND VALUABLES

While there may be something in the symbolic meanings of keys in the Viking Age, it is their practical functions that offer us glimpses at how power was exercised. The key itself betrays an ancient instinct to protect property. Viewed as functional objects – in close association with doors, boxes, chests and trunks – keys and locks were intimately linked to privacy, wealth and authority. They gave people the power to lock valuable objects away – to control their use – whether these be weapons, precious metals or even textiles.

Importantly, it was not just Viking women who owned keys: they also appear among the grave goods of men, as well as in settlement and urban sites where they are discovered as single finds. The surviving keys and their accompanying locks are enormously varied in design, but they are typically made of iron and copper alloys and would have required significant artistic and technical skill to produce.

A comparison of keys found at the sites of Gotland and Birka suggest that there may have been differences in the design and uses of men's and women's keys. Archaeologists have argued that keys buried with women tend to be much simpler and more functional, while men's keys on the whole have more ornate handles – some of which depict images of powerful birds – and more intricate tines or teeth. It is believed that, while women's keys tended to open doors – and so are connected with space and the home – men's were used for padlocks or chests, to secure weapons and valuables.

Birka

Situated on the Swedish island of Björkö – just off the coast of Stockholm, in Lake Mälaren – Birka was an important Viking city of between 500 and 1,000 inhabitants. Founded in around 750, it lasted for about 200 years until it was abandoned in 975. It is one of the most important archaeological sites in Scandinavia, and sheds crucial light on the development of Viking trading networks.

WEAPONS AND TREASURE

An astonishing number of fragments from around forty-four padlocks were found at Birka in Sweden, at the site of the fortified garrison building popularly known as the 'Hall of the Warriors'. Thousands of arrowheads were also found at the site, which further suggests its military connections, and hints that it came under sustained attack at some point. The padlocks were of Norse production and were used to protect this site, perhaps securing chests containing bows, swords, axes or arrows. From among the fragments are a number of smaller and weaker locks that would have been very easy to break, rather like the kind of locks on a modern-day secret diary. These smaller locks were probably ceremonial rather than for security – used where it was important to seal something symbolically. The question of who had access to the keys to these locks therefore became about power and hierarchy.

One of the finest examples of a locked Viking chest containing valuables comes from the Cuerdale Hoard. Discovered in the spring of 1840 on the banks of the River Ribble in Lancashire, the lead-lined chest contained some 7,500 silver coins and great quantities of other silver jewellery and scrap (or 'hack') silver. Around forty kilograms of silver in all, it is the largest-known Viking hoard in the West, and worldwide it is only surpassed by a handful of discoveries along the ancient Arabic silver route into Russia. The hoard, which dates from c.904, contains coins and jewellery from all over the Viking world: Scandinavia, Francia, Italy, Ireland, Pictland (now part of Scotland) and England. It is believed to be the loot of a Viking army, and its location in the north-west of Britain has led historians to link it to the expulsion of the Vikings from Dublin in 902, as some of them settled in what is now Lancashire.

·2·

GRAFFITI

Runes featuring Nordic names dating to the ninth century,
found in the Hagia Sophia, Istanbul

Graffiti is all about Viking travel...

Viking Age graffiti takes many forms – from rough marks, names and short phrases carved in runes, to complex symbols and pictures. In a world where paper was scarce, inscribing onto stone, wood or metal was an important form of literary expression – and, in combination with other sources, graffiti even enables us to study Viking travel around the world.

CONSTANTINOPLE

One of the most important sites of Viking graffiti is the mosque of Hagia Sophia in Istanbul (formerly Constantinople), which contains not only runic inscriptions but also images of four Viking ships dating from the second half of the ninth century to the early part of the tenth century. These carved markings testify to contact between Scandinavia and Byzantium, two giant maritime cultures of their time.

The Hagia Sophia

Built between 532 and 537 on the orders of the Byzantine emperor Justinian I, the Hagia Sophia (meaning 'Holy Wisdom') was an Eastern Orthodox Christian cathedral in Constantinople. The building's iconic central dome is more than fifty-five metres in height and more than thirty metres in diameter. It became a mosque in 1453, when Ottoman forces captured the city.

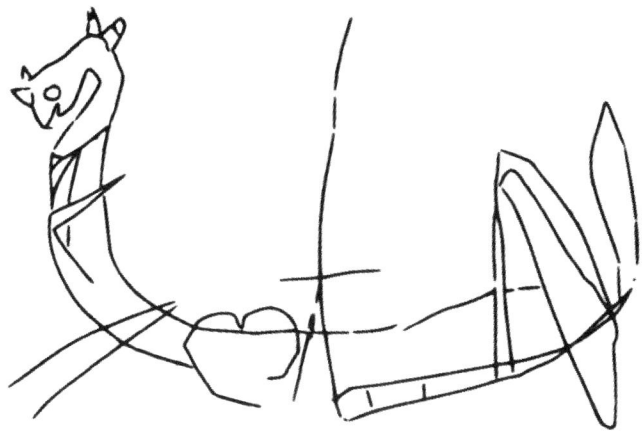

Sketch of a graffito of a Viking ship found in the Hagia Sophia

Scratched onto the walls of the second-storey aisles and galleries, the images clearly depict a variety of seagoing craft that are distinctly Viking in design – with long, narrow hulls – and are similar to ship graffiti discovered over 2,000 miles away in a church in Fortun, in the west of Norway. The most distinctive image is in the south gallery of the mosque, scratched onto the north-west column. It depicts a traditional longship with a dragon-head prow, which has been interpreted as a warship belonging to a wealthy man.

We know from archaeological and literary sources that there was indeed significant contact between Scandinavia and Byzantium from the ninth century onwards. Northerners (widely referred to as 'Varangians') made their way to the latter's capital city of Constantinople through the mediation of the Kievan Rus, and stayed to fight in the Byzantine army in their many wars against the Emirate of Crete and the Arabs in Syria. And they came in large numbers – in 988, Prince Vladimir of Kiev sent no fewer than 6,000 Vikings as military muscle to fight for the Byzantine emperor, Basil II. This force later formed the core of the Varangian Guard, a fearsome band of troops whose role was to defend the emperor.

The Kievan Rus

A loose confederation of tribes under Scandinavian rule who inhabited an area between the Baltic and Black seas between c.880 and c.1240, with the main power base in Kiev. At its height, the majority of the East Slavic tribes were united under the Rus.

It is entirely possible that another set of graffiti, found on the top floor of the south gallery of the Hagia Sophia, was made by two of these soldiers. Inscribed in a runic alphabet on a parapet are two Viking men's names: Halvdan and Are. Such isolated examples are difficult to make sense of, but here the graffiti is potent evidence of a Viking presence – and quite possibly a heathen Viking presence – in what was one of the holiest churches in Christendom.

The presence of graffiti in such a significant holy site can be interpreted in a number of ways. Firstly, it suggests that the Hagia Sophia had a magnet-like importance as a tourist attraction for foreigners in the tenth century, just as it does today. Secondly, there is a long tradition of graffiti as a form of invocation in holy sites, and it may be that – in carving ships onto the walls – seafarers were hoping for a safe voyage. Thirdly, given the length of Orthodox religious services, graffiti may simply have been an act of diversion to while away the hours, a pure expression of Viking boredom.

A BYZANTINE LION

Another surviving example of Viking graffiti is scratched into a marble statue of a lion, one of four beasts that today guard the Arsenal in Venice. The lion, however, is not Venetian; it was originally located in the Athenian port of Piraeus, which during the Viking Age was part of the Byzantine empire. The lion was looted by Venetian troops in 1687 during the Great Turkish War, and was taken home by the naval commander – and later Doge of Venice – Francesco Morosini (1619–94) as a war trophy.

The graffiti takes the form of two long runic phrases, twisting in the shape of a serpentine dragon curled around the lion's shoulder. Although the writing has now faded to the extent that it is impossible to decipher, several earlier attempts were made. The inscriptions were first recognized as runes in the eighteenth century by the Swedish diplomat Johan David Åkerblad. The first translation was made in 1854 by Carl Christian Rafn, the secretary of the Royal Society of Nordic Antiquaries, and another attempt was made by Eric Brate in 1914, which is widely considered the most accurate. Thought to have been carved by Varangian Guards, the graffiti appears to celebrate the exploits of a great warrior:

> They cut him down in the midst of his
> forces. But in the harbour the men cut
> runes by the sea in memory of Horsi, a
> good warrior.
> The Swedes set this on the lion.
> He went his way with good counsel,
> gold he won in his travels.

GIMME SHELTER

One of the most impressive collections of Viking graffiti outside of Scandinavia can be found on the Scottish island of Orkney. A Viking territory for very nearly 600 years, from 875 to 1468, and directly on the route west from Scandinavia – to Iceland, Scotland, Ireland, the Isle of Man and the west coast of northern

England – Orkney was in the middle of the principal northern Viking maritime highway.

The graffiti survives in a curious place, a Neolithic chambered tomb named Maeshowe. Built almost 5,000 years ago, the tomb is an enormous mound measuring over thirty-five metres in diameter and standing over seven metres high. It is designed so that the light of the setting sun highlights the entrance passageway during the winter solstice. The graffiti was discovered in 1861, when the mound was first excavated.

The tomb itself is referred to as 'Orkahaugr' in *Orkneyinga saga*, which describes how, in the winter of 1153, Earl Harald took shelter in the ancient burial chamber during a snowstorm:

> On the thirteenth day of Christmas they travelled on foot over to Firth. During a snowstorm they took shelter in Orkahaugr [Maeshowe] and two of them (his men) went insane which slowed them down badly so that by the time they reached Firth it was night time.

It is perfectly possible that, while shut inside the tomb, these Norsemen carved their names into its walls during the long stormy night.

The walls of Maeshowe are covered with around thirty examples of runic graffiti, which range from the light-hearted to the erotic. A large number are little more than personal names –

Orkneyinga saga

Also known as the *History of the Earls of Orkney*, this saga narrates the history of Orkney and Shetland and their interactions with Norway and Scotland. It begins by outlining the takeover of the islands by Harald Fairhair, before recounting the lives of subsequent earls (or *jarls*).

'Ofram the son of Sigurd carved these runes', 'Haermund Hardaxe carved these runes', 'Tryggr carved these runes' – the Viking equivalent of modern-day tagging. More bombastic is the phrase 'These runes were carved by the man most skilled in runes in the western ocean'.

Among the more idiosyncratic examples are the sexually explicit inscriptions, which have been translated as 'Thorni fucked. Helgi carved' and 'Ingigerth is the most beautiful of all women', a declaration which appears beside an image of a slobbering dog. Others speak of treasure hidden and carried away. At least one of the inscriptions relates to travel: 'Thatir the Viking came here to weary', which conjures up an image of the fatigue that came with seafaring. The Vikings journeyed far beyond Scandinavia in their open boats – and quite literally left their mark wherever they went.

·3·

NICKNAMES

Coin of Erik Bloodaxe. It reads ERIC REX ('King Eric')

*Viking nicknames are all about
everyday life…*

A WORLD OF NAMES

A wonderful world of Viking nicknames has survived the centuries. There are traces in the thirteenth-century Icelandic sagas, the residue of names passed along the centuries via oral tradition; names are carved in runic inscriptions and Viking graffiti; and they are even embedded in our modern world as place names, signs of Viking migration and settlement. Interestingly, however, there is a marked imbalance between the plentiful examples of nicknames for men and the scarcity of nicknames for women, which may reflect the dominant role played by men within society and their ability to name and be named.

Such nicknames are a treasure trove of information. They open a window onto everyday speech, slang, popular culture, humour and – of the most interest to a historian – can even shed light on an individual's history, because nicknames are so often created from moments in one's past.

As a Viking you might be named, for example, for your distinctive clothing, like Ragnarr loðbrók – Ragnar Furry-trousers – who was so-called on account of the animal-skin trousers made for him by his wife. You might be named for characteristics such as generosity, like Þórdís todda – Thordis Gift-giver – who always gave generously to the poor. You might be named for a disability, like Ívarr hinn beinlausi (Ivar the Boneless), a nickname believed by some historians to refer to a genetic illness affecting his skeleton. And the list goes on, covering a wide cross-section of Viking life: religious beliefs, occupation, social position, specific events, praise, insults, the natural world, family origin and mythology. The mythical Swedish king Erik

Väderhatt (Erik Weatherhat), for example, was known for his powers over the weather and direction – which he could influence by turning around his hat.

There were even nicknames relating to sex or one's genitalia. Herjólfr hrokkineista (meaning 'shrivelled testicle') must have been named for his imperfect organs; Erlendr bakrauf ('back-hole') was presumably named for some bottom-related feat or misdemeanour; Eysteinn meinfretr ('harm-fart') was likely named for his facility for flatulence; and Ásmundr kastandrazi was 'throwing ass' (read this as 'hip-thruster'), suggesting a certain vigour. Perhaps most oddly, Kolbeinn smjorreðr was named 'butter penis' for... well, it's not entirely clear, though we do know that the Vikings used the word 'butter' to suggest wealth or plenty – for to make butter you need good cattle and good land.

PERSONAL HISTORIES

A person's nickname could even have its own history, because names could change over time: Haraldr lúfa was named for his appearance – *lúfa* meaning 'shaggy-head', after his thick hair like a shock of wheat – but was then *re*named Haraldr hárfagri (Harald Fairhair) when he finally washed and cut it after a decade.

It was also possible to have two nicknames in one, such as *holtaskalli* – meaning 'baldy from Holtar' – just as it was possible to have two entirely separate nicknames. In the *Laxdæla saga*, a man with a perfectly good second name, Án svarti (Án the Black), is given another when he reveals a dream that does not portray him in his best light as a warrior. After a night of 'great amusement and joy', Án drifted into a difficult slumber in which he dreamt of a 'repulsive' woman who came to him with a sword in one hand and a tray in the other. She pulled him to the floor, slit open his belly, tore out his entrails and replaced them with brushwood. When he recounts this tale, his friends hoot with laughter and say that he should now be called Án hrísmagi ('brushwood-belly'). In this way, nicknames were an important part of Viking humour, and were also used to tease and mock.

Detailed descriptions of *how* Vikings got their nicknames are quite rare, however. In the sagas, characters are usually just introduced by name rather than with a backstory, but occasionally we do find out why a particular epithet stuck. Consider, for example, the tenth-century Norwegian ruler Erik Haraldsson, who was known as Erik Bloodaxe. In *Egil's saga* we have one explanation of how he got his nickname:

> Gunnhildr, his wife, was of all women the most beautiful; a woman small of stature yet great of counsel. She became so wicked in her counsel, and he so easily led to acts cruel and oppressive to the people, that it was hard to bear. He had killed his brother Óláfr digrbeinn ('thick-legged') and Bjǫrn and others of his brothers. Thus he was called blóðøx, because he was a cruel and ruthless man, and mostly as a result of her counsel.

Erik Bloodaxe (d.954)

Erik Haraldsson – or Erik Bloodaxe – was a Viking leader and ruler of Northumbria, and the son of Harald Fairhair, the first King of Norway. He appears very clearly as a character in sagas, but is a somewhat faint figure in the tenth-century records. Nonetheless, he was thought to have twice ruled Northumbria, in 947–8 and 952–4, and issued coinage, a particularly fine example of which is in the collections of the British Museum.

Here the story is clear: Erik received his name for his violence and ruthlessness, and for the ease with which he would wet his axe with anyone's blood – even that of his closest kin. Erik's violence is also linked here with ambition. As one of several sons of the King of Norway, murdering his brothers secured Erik the throne. His reign lasted just five years – from c.929 to c.934 – before yet another brother came along and drove him out of Norway.

A LONG LIFE

While the Vikings' motivation for giving each other nicknames is still poorly understood, there is some evidence that offers a hint as to naming practices, such as the story of a young man named Helgi who earns the nickname Spike (*broddr*) to become Brodd-Helgi. We know from his appearance in the *Vápnfirðinga saga* that in his early years this handsome youth was overbearing and headstrong, tricky and capricious – and, in one of the splendid touches so common in the sagas that speak clearly to us in the present day, that he was 'not much of a talker'.

Keen to be a man of deeds rather than words, the young Helgi acquired his name when two bulls – one old and large, and another young and keen – began to butt each other as the cows stood around in the milking pen. The younger bull clearly began to lose the fight, but Helgi intervened on its behalf and cleverly (and bravely) attached an iron spike to its head. Thus unicorned, the young bull won the fight and no doubt the prize of several cows.

The saga then continues with an important line:

He received the nickname from this event that he was called Brodd-Helgi, and back then it seemed to people greatly promising to have two names. At that time, it was people's belief that those people who had two names would live longer.

Nicknames, therefore, could hold considerable symbolic value, and it is no surprise that the giving and receiving of a nickname was sometimes a formal process – in which it was attached to an individual, along with the giving of a gift, as part of a 'name-fastening' ceremony. It is this formal recognition of such names by the Vikings, a reflection of their importance in society, that has led to their survival over the centuries, allowing so many glimpses into everyday life.

·4·

MISCHIEF

———

Loki, the Viking god of mischief, depicted in an
eighteenth-century Icelandic manuscript

*Viking mischief is all about the
power of the gods…*

A GOD OF MISCHIEF

The Vikings loved a troublemaker, and even had a god of mischief – the shape-shifting pedlar of unrest, Loki. Scholars argue in minutiae over his characteristics because of the difficulty of translating from Old Norse into English, but he is most commonly associated with the word *læ*. Few of the translations of this term are complimentary, and all relate to Loki's slyness. They include:

> Craft... art... skill... fraud... treason... harm... bane... evil... woe... misfortune... ruin.

Perhaps he is described best, though, by the Icelandic scholar Snorri Sturluson. In the *Prose Edda*, the first systematic survey of Old Norse mythology, written or compiled around 1220, Sturluson describes Loki as 'maker of mischiefs, the cunning *áss*, calumniator and tricker of the gods'.

Snorri Sturluson (1179–1241)

One of the most interesting characters of the Viking Age. An Icelandic poet, historian and chieftain, he is the author of the *Prose Edda* and *Heimskringla*, two of the most important Icelandic sagas. In 1215-18 and 1222-32 he was also the lawspeaker – or president – of the Icelandic Althing (parliament).

Loki could switch gender – he spent eight winters beneath the earth as a woman milking cows – and he could even switch species: in the sagas he transforms into a fly, a salmon and a bird on separate occasions. This ability to shapeshift between forms and identities in order to inveigle himself into certain situations gave him a unique ability to wreak havoc and mischief.

Loki's exploits are numerous, not least of which is the fact that he was single-handedly responsible for killing Odin's son Baldr, who was praised and loved by all. Baldr was also a god and was associated with good things – light, joy, purity and the summer sun – and he was impervious to anything apart from mistletoe. Loki heard of this, made a spear (or perhaps an arrow) from mistletoe and gave it to Baldr's brother, the blind god Hodr. Not knowing what he had in his hands, and joining in with some tomfoolery among the gods, Hodr unintentionally killed Baldr with the mistletoe spear.

For this crime, Loki was given a punishment which must rank as one of the most imaginative in history: he was bound – with the guts of his own son acting as ropes – to three sharp rocks, while a snake, suspended above him, dripped poison onto his face. Needless to say, Loki escaped to carry on his life of destruction.

If the slaying of Odin's son was his most far-reaching act, one of his most mischievous was the cutting of Sif's hair. Sif was the wife of Thor, the god of thunder. A dangerous target you might think; but not so for Loki, who not only claimed that Sif had had an affair with him, but then cut off her beautiful golden hair for which she was renowned – and he did so for no apparent reason other than the opportunity presented itself while she slept.

Possessed by a thunderous rage, Thor vowed to break every bone in Loki's body, and only reneged upon his deadly threat when Loki promised to make her an even finer head of hair. He did this by travelling to the land of the dwarves – the greatest craftsmen in the worlds of gods or man – where the Sons of Ivaldi made her new hair from strands of gold.

GIFTS BORN OF MISCHIEF

Not only was Loki forced to make Sif a new head of golden hair, but he also had to offer Thor and other gods enchanted gifts of reconciliation. Out of this new partnership between Loki and the dwarves came nothing less than Thor's hammer, Mjölnir, forged by the brothers Sindri and Brokkr.

The story of the making of magical gifts for the gods by Sindri and Brokkr is relayed in Snorri Sturluson's *Prose Edda*, which makes it clear that by no means is it incidental that these most powerful of Viking treasures were born of mischief. Loki literally bet his head that the two brothers could not make gifts for the gods as beautiful as those made by the Sons of Ivaldi, which included Odin's spear and the god Freyr's magical boat *Skíðblaðnir*, a vessel that could be folded up small enough to be placed into a pocket.

The brothers accepted the challenge and began to work, with Brokkr being given strict instructions by his brother to work the bellows non-stop to keep the forge at the right temperature – while Sindri made a boar for Freyr which had bristles on its back that glowed in the dark, a ring for Odin which multiplied itself eight times every ninth night, and finally Thor's hammer, Mjölnir.

Mjölnir

According to Norse mythology, Mjölnir is the famous hammer given to Thor by Loki. Forged by dwarves, it was said to be capable of levelling mountains, and it would never fail, never miss and would always return to Thor's hand when thrown. It was made, however, with an imperfection: its short handle meant that it could only be wielded with one hand.

During the forging, Loki appeared in a typically impish manner, disguised as a fly which bit Brokkr in an attempt to put him off his task. On the first two occasions – while the boar and the ring were being forged – he managed to keep working despite the irritating Loki-fly, but the third bite drew blood, which dripped into his eyes and made him momentarily take his hands off the bellows. At this point, Sindri took the hammer out of the fire to find that the handle was too short: thus Loki had managed to sabotage the forging of Thor's hammer.

THE ARCHAEOLOGY OF MISCHIEF

There is even an archaeology of mischief, as Loki has been discovered on something known as the 'Snaptun Stone', a semicircular piece of soapstone found on a beach near Snaptun in Denmark in 1950. Carved around 1000 CE, the face on the stone has been identified as Loki because of the numerous vertical marks that cross his lips – believed to be stitches and scars that relate to the story of that bet with the two dwarf brothers.

Sketch of the 'Snaptun Stone' carved c.1000, depicting the
Norse god Loki's lips sewn up

Despite the misshapen hammer handle, Loki lost the bet with Brokkr, and the dwarf tried to claim his prize by decapitating Loki. Unperturbed, Loki argued that his neck was not part of the wager, and therefore he should not lose his head. Brokkr accepted the point but, claiming that Loki's head was his to do with as he pleased, he sewed the god's lips shut with an awl and a leather thong, which 'tore the edges off' his lips, thus quietening Loki's dangerous tongue. But, as ever with Loki, he broke his lip-bonds (by tearing his mouth open) and set off again, a tornado of trouble.

There is more to the Snaptun Stone than a simple carved face, however. Just below the mouth is a hole, and there is another in the centre of the head; it is believed that the stone functioned as a hearthstone or blast nozzle for a forge. By blowing air with bellows into the hole by the mouth, flames would erupt out of the top of the figure's head, a powerful reminder that yet another of Loki's identities was as a god of fire.

THE KILLING OF KING EDMUND

The sense of Viking mischief found in the sagas and misadventures of Loki was not confined to the page, but was also evident in real-life situations. One such occasion occurred on the battlefield in 869, when King Edmund of East Anglia and his forces were defeated by the Great Heathen Army led by Ivar the Boneless.

Once in Viking hands, Edmund was taunted and mocked before suffering a humiliating death for refusing to renounce Christ. The account of his martyrdom survives in a tenth-century account of his life by the French monk Abbo of Fleury. In it, we are told of how King Edmund was bound, insulted 'ignominiously' and beaten with rods:

> afterwards [Ivar] led the devout king to a firm living tree, and tied him there with strong bonds, and beat him with whips. In between the whip lashes, Edmund called out

with true belief in the Saviour Christ. Because of his belief, because he called to Christ to aid him, the heathens became furiously angry. They then shot spears at him, as if it was a game, until he was entirely covered with their missiles, like the bristles of a hedgehog.

After the target practice had taken place, Edmund was cut down and beheaded, at which point – we are told – 'his soul journeyed happily to Christ'. Even in the bloodiness of battle, cruelty and torture were mixed with ridicule and horseplay, and in it the Vikings found opportunities for mischief.

The Great Heathen Army

The name given by the Anglo-Saxons to a large coalition of Vikings who invaded in 865, intent on conquering the seven Anglo-Saxon kingdoms – Wessex, Mercia, Northumbria, Kent, Essex, Sussex and East Anglia. In 866 they captured York, which remained a Viking city for eighty-eight years. Subsequent campaigns led to a large part of England falling under Viking rule, which became known as the 'Danelaw'.

·5·

HAIR GROOMING

Hair from the tenth-century cremation grave on Adelsö Island,
Sweden, now in the Swedish History Museum

*Viking hair grooming is all
about social boundaries...*

The history of Viking grooming and hair is difficult to uncover in the historical and archaeological record, since so few sources actually survive from the period. Nonetheless, through an imaginative reading of textual, pictorial and archaeological sources – including examples of combs and even, in rare cases, tufts of real hair – the world of the hirsute emerges to display a bewilderingly complex range of meanings and cultural practices.

Throughout the Viking Age, grooming practices associated with hair and hairstyles were an important way of marking Viking social boundaries. People of certain social groups, gender, occupations, ages and ethnicities could be identified by the look of their hair and the way in which it was worn. Long hair denoted beauty and virtue, with Viking women almost universally favouring the ponytail; greying or white hair was associated with wisdom, old age and authority; to be unable to grow facial hair or to be clean-shaven as a man was a sign of effeminacy; and Scandinavian hairstyles appear to have been strong ethnic symbols that distinguished them from their enemies.

HAIR GROOMING AND FEAR

Evidence for a distinctively Viking hairstyle can be glimpsed among the thinly scattered sources that shed light on hair grooming. Hair was one way in which the Vikings' foes singled them out as different, foreign, and ultimately as dangerous.

A specifically Scandinavian hairstyle is referred to in a passage from an early Christian Norwegian regional legal code, which stated that, should a drowned seafarer with a Norse hairstyle be washed ashore, he was to receive a Christian burial. And the cleric Alcuin wrote to King Æthelred of Northumbria in 793, warning him of the pagan Vikings: 'Are not these the people whose terror threatens us, yet you want to copy their hair?' This Christian writer railed about the destructive savagery of these Norsemen – but interestingly he identified this pagan threat by the styling of their hair.

Others were also wary of the grooming habits of the Vikings. The English author of the Chronicle of John of Wallingford was concerned about the sexual attractiveness of the incoming Danes of the tenth and eleventh centuries, who he considered:

> caused much trouble to the natives of the land; for they were wont, after the fashion of their country, to comb their hair every day, to bathe every Saturday, to change their garments often, and set off their persons by many frivolous devices. In this matter they laid siege to the virtue of the married woman, and persuaded the daughters even of the noble to be their concubines.

John of Wallingford (d. 1258)

A Benedictine monk at the Abbey of St Albans, who was in charge of the infirmary of the abbey in the last decade of his life. He is widely associated with a miscellaneous manuscript known as the 'Chronicle of John of Wallingford' in the British Library, compiled in the third quarter of the thirteenth century. In addition to containing a chronicle of English history from 1 CE to 1258 CE, the manuscript also includes an early description and drawing of an elephant.

Well-dressed Vikings with kempt hair were thus viewed as a threat to English men. Scandinavian hair grooming was therefore not only distinctive, defining them as a group, but also threatening: these were fearsome warriors and seducers.

THE IDENTITY OF COMBS

The subject of Viking hair is intricately connected to the objects associated with grooming. These include shears and razors, and small knives for shaving and trimming hair, but by far the most common of such archaeological finds are combs.

Combs facilitated the styling of hair, which in turn asserted social and national boundaries, but they were also about identity – either the identity of the comb-maker or of the individual object's owner. An eleventh-century comb – now in the collections of the British Museum after being dug up at a site near Lincoln in 1851 – bears a rare inscription of the maker, which translates as 'A good comb Thorfastr made'. Combs were ordinarily made of bone or antler – difficult and time-consuming materials to work with that demanded both a high level of skill and a range of specialist tools. Comb-makers such as Thorfastr would have been craftsmen of immense skill, and this inscription may well have functioned as an advertisement of his particular talent.

Experimental archaeologists who have reconstructed the making of Viking combs estimate that it must have taken a whole day or more to produce a single item. The process involved the sourcing, treatment and cutting of the antler and removal of the porous core, before the comb was then shaped – often in numerous parts or sections – and decorated. The component parts were then assembled, with separate pieces drilled and riveted together with iron or copper alloy – comb-making required specialist techniques not only in working with bone, but also with metal. The back of the comb was then levelled, and only at this stage were the teeth cut and shaped. Finally, the finished product was polished, ready to be sold. Still its identity was not complete, however, for now its appearance could be adapted by its new owner, who might alter the design or add personal inscriptions or graffiti.

A WORLD OF COMBS

The fact that combs were made of hard-wearing materials such as bone or antler means that numerous examples have survived. In fact, combs are one of the most common archaeological objects of the entire Viking Age, with the site of Hedeby at the southern end of the Jutland peninsula producing an amazing *340,000* fragments of comb.

The survival of so many combs from the ninth and tenth centuries – both ornate examples for the wealthy and more rudimentary designs for non-elite consumption – indicates that, once comb-making technology had been devised and mastered, it proliferated widely, and also that a grooming culture was increasingly accessible at different levels of Viking society.

While the use of combs to style hair marked out clear boundaries between different groups, the simple fact of owning a comb did not. Combs were owned by both men and women, and were often kept on one's person – either worn on the belt or placed in a cover of bone or in a leather purse as a fashion statement. It is no coincidence that a number of legendary Viking leaders were known by hair-related sobriquets, including Harald Fairhair, Erik the Red and Svein Forkbeard.

Svein Forkbeard (960–1014)

King of Denmark from 986 to 1014, having revolted against his father Harald Bluetooth and usurped the throne. His children included King Harald II of Denmark, King Cnut the Great and Queen Estrid Svendsdatter – who gave her name to the dynasty that ruled Denmark from 1047 until 1412. Svein's power extended well beyond Denmark, and he ruled most of Norway after 1000. In 1013, just before his death, he became the first Danish King of England.

HAIR THEFT

Throughout most cultures in the past, hair has achieved an extraordinary significance, so intimately connected is it with the body and an individual's identity. It can be worn long or short, be plaited or otherwise decorated or styled, and it can be dyed or have a naturally distinctive colour. It constantly grows – even shortly after death – but it may also thin or fall out entirely. Hair can be cut painlessly but is painful when pulled or torn out, and to cut or yank it out without the owner's permission is widely viewed as a violation of that person's body.

Think here of that old trickster Loki, who cut off the long golden hair of Thor's wife Sif, whose lustrous locks were a defining part of her famed beauty (see p. 33). By cutting Sif's hair, Loki was both committing an act of violation against her and interfering with another man's wife – in this case a god's, and not just any god but the god of thunder. In committing this crime, Loki crossed a boundary that no one else would even have considered testing.

·6·
HOT SPRINGS AND SAUNAS

The hot bath at Snorri Sturluson's farm at Reykholt in Iceland

Viking hot springs and saunas are all about love and murder…

HOT SPRINGS

There is good evidence that the Vikings bathed in hot springs and baths that were specially built to take advantage of nearby geothermal activity. One of the finest surviving examples is in Reykholt in western Iceland, where the poet and chieftain Snorri Sturluson had his farm. The bath nestles in a slight hollow surrounded by flat stones on all sides. An underground passageway ran from the house directly to the pool, allowing easy access for relaxation and bathing.

Records show that Snorri's bath was already in use when he moved to the farm in 1204, taking over the residence from Reverend Magnús Pálsson – whose father had served Reykholt before him. The bath's origin, therefore, may lie far deeper in Viking history than Snorri's time. The first written mention of a pool in the area, possibly Snorri's bath itself, is in *Land-námabók*, an Icelandic chronicle which describes in detail the Norse settlement of Iceland in 915. The bath was lost to history during the Middle Ages but reappeared in 1724, when it was described by the Icelandic poet Páll Vídalín, and then again in 1817, when Icelandic priests were required to record information on archaeological remains in their parishes and send it to the Royal Commission in Denmark. The then priest at Reykholt, the Reverend Eggert Guðmundsson, accordingly sent a detailed description of the pool. In the centuries since, it has undergone several reconstructions, though the features are believed to have been faithful to the original arrangement. These include seats below the waterline around the circumference, and the underground passageway to the farm.

Hints of the existence of other hot pools in the Viking period come from local place names that – like Snorri's Reykholt – feature the element *reyk-* (from *reykr*, meaning 'smoke' or 'steam'). The most famous of these is the Icelandic capital, Reykjavík, which was built in an area of Iceland blessed with geothermal activity.

MURDER IN THE STEAM ROOM

There is also evidence that the Vikings built saunas which, unlike the hot baths, would not have been restricted to areas of geothermal activity.

One of the most detailed descriptions comes from *Eyrbyggja saga*, in which a man named Styr tries to rid himself of some troublesome Berserkers, legendary Norse warriors who fought with the utmost ferocity and entered the battlefield in a state of wild fury. Berserkers feature a great deal in the Icelandic sagas, which depict them as having superhuman strength – often fighting without armour, biting their shields and striking fear into the hearts of their enemies. Styr's problem is that a Berserker named Halli has seduced his daughter and proposed marriage. A steam room is central to the extraordinarily convoluted and violent plot that subsequently unravels, and it provides an unrivalled picture of what a Viking sauna was actually like.

Eyrbyggja saga

Icelandic saga also known as *The Saga of the People of Eyri*, it focuses on a long-running feud between two chieftains, Snorri Goði and Arnkel Goði. It is particularly valuable for its descriptions of Viking rituals and superstitions, and of voyages to Greenland and North America.

Styr grudgingly promises to allow Halli to marry his daughter, but only if the Berserkers complete a number of exhausting tasks – including nothing less than clearing a road through a lava field. While Halli and his men slave away at these tasks, Styr has a steam room built and it is well described.

The room is constructed partially below ground level and is accessed via a trap door. It is heated by a stone-lined stove, and above the stove is a window that allows water to be poured onto the fire, creating steam. We can assume that its design is effective, since the saga tells us how 'wondrous hot was that place'.

The story takes a turn when Styr's daughter, decked in her finest clothes, walks past Halli after he is done with work for the day. He takes the opportunity to recite some splendid poetry, a window into Viking flirting:

> Where are you going,
> Gerd of the forearm's fire,
> walking past so elegantly
> – never lie to me linen-decked one –
> for I have never seen you
> dressed in such splendour,
> walking from the house this winter,
> wise goddess of table-games.

It is not made explicitly clear exactly what Styr thinks of this, but the subsequent events have more than a hint of pre-planned murder about them. That evening, he suggests to the Berserkers, who are exhausted from their immense labours, that they enjoy his sauna. Then, having lured them in, he piles stones onto the hatch, trapping them inside, and adds water to the fire via the window. This makes the bathhouse so hot that the Berserkers rush at the door.

Halli manages to escape, breaking through the trap door, but Styr has prepared for that eventuality by placing a wet cow's hide on the stairs leading down from the bathhouse. When Halli bursts outside, therefore, he slips and falls, upon which Styr 'gave him his death-wound', and when another tries to rush out, Styr 'thrust a spear through him and he fell back into the bath-house and died there'.

LOVE IN THE BATHS

The Vikings did not just use their bathing facilities to murder people, however. Baths feature throughout *Laxdœla saga*, an account of the lives of the earliest generations of settlers who came to Iceland, in a very different context.

Laxdæla saga

Written in Iceland in the thirteenth century, this saga tells the story of families in the Breiðafjörður area in the west of the country, during the late ninth to early eleventh centuries. It focuses largely on the childhood friends Kjartan Ólafsson and Bolli Þorleiksson, who come to blows when they both fall in love with the same woman, Guðrún Ósvífursdóttir.

Guðrún, the female heroine (who, importantly for historians, was great-grandmother to Iceland's first vernacular chronicler and historian, Ari Þorgilsson), lives on a farm called Laugar – which literally means 'baths' – being so named for the hot springs there. The saga records how the springs are a focus of daily community life, used for bathing, laundry, cooking and socializing.

The saga includes the most vivid love triangle of all of the Viking sagas, and it begins in a hot spring. In this story, the twice-widowed Guðrún meets her new love, Kjartan, at the baths in Sælingdalur in the west of Iceland, and they go on to meet there repeatedly. Although things start well, with 'Kjartan and Guðrún thought to be the best matched', soon Kjartan's foster brother and closest friend, Bolli, also becomes emotionally involved with Guðrún.

It does not end well. What begins as harmless flirting in the natural pool leads to the deaths of both Kjartan (ambushed and murdered by Bolli) and Bolli (decapitated by one of Kjartan's brothers in the dairy at Sælingdalur), and sows salt on their family relationships for generations, fuelled by Guðrún's endless capacity for hatred and revenge.

CLEAN OR DIRTY?

Bathing had another effect on the Vikings: it made them attractive to the Anglo-Saxons. A writer whose words are often credited to John of Wallingford (d.1258) – a monk at the Abbey of St Albans – recorded in a preface to his description of the St Brice's Day Massacre of 13 November 1002 how Anglo-Saxon women found the Norse men attractive because 'unlike Anglo-Saxon men, they combed their hair daily, took baths weekly, and laundered their clothing regularly'.

St Brice's Day Massacre of 1002

A massacre of Danes in England by the English king, Æthelred the Unready – possibly a response to a threat against the king's life. It is unclear how many Danes were killed or how widespread the killings were, but the *Anglo-Saxon Chronicle* is clear that he 'ordered slain all the Danish men who were in England'.

Supporting evidence for such regular washing comes from the East. Preserved in a document known as the *Russian Primary Chronicle* are the texts of various treaties agreed between the Byzantine empire and Vikings from Sweden and the East Baltic area. A treaty of 907 contained a clause requiring the Byzantines not only to give the Rus merchants food, drink and supplies for their ships, but also to provide baths 'as often as they want them'.

The Viking approach to cleanliness was not attractive to everyone that they met, however. Ahmad ibn Fadlan, the Muslim diplomat and writer from Baghdad who had first-hand experience of Vikings who traded around the Caspian Sea and on the Volga River, was impressed by their appearance – 'I have never seen more perfect physiques than theirs – they are like palm trees, are fair and reddish, and do not wear the tunic or the caftan' – but what really caught his attention was their approach to grooming, which he abhorred. Writing in the tenth century, he said:

> Every day they must wash their faces and heads and this they do in the dirtiest and filthiest fashion possible: to wit, every morning a girl servant brings a great basin of water; she offers this to her master and he washes his hands and face and his hair – he washes it and combs it out with a comb in the water; then he blows his nose and spits into the basin. When he has finished, the servant carries the basin to the next person, who does likewise. She carries the basin thus to all the household in turn, and each blows his nose, spits, and washes his face and hair in it.

He was also appalled at how 'they are the filthiest of all Allah's creatures: they do not purify themselves after excreting or urinating or wash themselves when in a state of ritual impurity after coitus and do not even wash their hands after food'.

Concepts of cleanliness and attitudes towards 'dirt' are culturally and historically relative, of course. Daily ablutions for the Rus were a communal rather than a private activity, which probably contributed to the revulsion of this diplomat from the Abbasid Caliphate. And the sharing of washing-water teeming with other people's spit and snot would be distasteful to our modern standards, too.

·7·

BREAK-INS

The ninth-century Oseberg Ship in situ during its excavation, 1904–5.
It soon became clear that the grave mound had already been entered
and its contents tampered with

*Break-ins are all about Viking
power politics...*

A striking feature of Viking Age burials is that there is often evidence of subsequent break-ins and destruction. Those who did the breaking-in sometimes even left behind the tools they used – such as spades and stretchers to remove soil and grave goods – which can be dated scientifically to prove that many interventions took place only a few generations after the grave was first sealed.

One of the modern-day misconceptions about breaking into Viking Age burial mounds is that it was done simply to plunder the riches that were deposited as grave goods alongside the bones of the deceased. While for some, robbing from graves for material gain may have been an overriding consideration, in other cases this explanation of treasure-seeking is too simplistic. Sometimes objects were taken not because of their material value but because of the powers that they were thought to possess.

MAGIC SWORDS

Swords and pieces of jewellery were considered special objects during the Viking Age, and were passed on as gifts and heirlooms. In some instances they were given names, or even thought to have supernatural or magical properties. Where individuals were buried with such precious items, the burial sites may have been reopened in order to acquire them.

In most cases the archaeological evidence for plundering such weapons of power is slim, though a case can be made from the *lack* of traditional grave goods of this type in certain graves where one would have expected them to be buried. In the instance of a grave in Gulli, just outside of Tønsberg in Norway, a reopened grave was discovered with the hilt of a weapon, but no blade; the latter, it is assumed, was carried off. Of six other graves thought to have been reopened at this site, one contained many grave goods but no jewellery or weapons, which had also, presumably, been taken away upon reopening.

The significance of certain weapons can be found in Old Norse written sources, which speak of the potency and power of legendary Viking weaponry. The sagas identify at least two clear motives for breaking into graves. The first is to gain secret knowledge; the second is to acquire a named sword, ring or helmet that has particular powers.

One of the most famous named Viking swords was Sköfnung, which belonged to the legendary Danish king Hrólf Kraki. It was renowned for its sharpness and toughness, since it was said to be imbued with the spirits of the king's dozen Berserker bodyguards. The Icelandic *Landnámabók* tells of how the warrior Midfjords-Skegge broke into the grave of Hrólf and took the blade, the ownership of which gave him great power and respect among his peers. Swords of this nature, whether real or legendary, became heirlooms, passed from one generation to the next. Thus Sköfnung passed from Midfjords-Skegge to his son Eid, who lent it to his kinsman Thorkel Eyjólfsson in order to fight and kill the outlaw Grim.

BREAKING THE BONES OF THE DEAD

In other examples, the ship burials at Oseberg and Gokstad in particular, archaeologists have observed that some objects in graves were not taken but intentionally smashed and destroyed. When viewed in the context of Viking Age culture, it is believed that this represents a form of domination and power politics.

Oseberg ship burial

A burial mound in Oseberg, Norway, first excavated in 1904–5, which has been dated by dendrochronology to the autumn of 834. It contained the best-preserved Viking ship ever discovered, two female skeletons, and a treasure of grave goods including wooden sleighs, bed-posts and chests, as well as the only known Viking Age cart. It is now on display at the Viking Ship Museum in Oslo.

In Oseberg it is the attitude towards the remains of the bodies that is most interesting. The grave contained the bones of two women: one older, one younger. Most of the bones of the older woman had been removed from the burial chamber and scattered in the trench dug by the intruder to break into the grave but the actual bones from the face were missing. Historians believe this to be especially significant – evidence of a violent act against the very identity of the dead.

As for the younger woman, very few bones survived, though some were scattered in the access trench as well as in the burial chamber. Fragments of her cranium were found in both places, suggesting that the skull had been intentionally crushed. It appears that the majority of the younger woman's skeleton was then removed from the mound by the intruders.

Similarly, in the famous Gokstad ship burial there is evidence of a break-in, and here too the bones appear to have been removed or otherwise destroyed. The body of a man in his forties or fifties was interred in the mound, but in the grave chamber itself only a handful of bones survive; others were scattered in the access trench – including four leg bones, a shoulder blade, an arm bone and only fragments of skull. This suggests that, like at Oseberg, the intruders consciously smashed the skull of the interred body.

In each case there was also intentional damage inflicted upon the physical structure of the ship itself. Intruders appear to have removed a two-metre ornamental part of the stern of the Oseberg vessel, and key sections of the Gokstad ship's bottom and sides were cut away.

Gokstad ship burial

A ninth-century burial mound in Gokstad which was discovered in 1880, it contained the largest preserved Viking ship ever found in Norway. The grave goods included three smaller boats, a tent, a sledge and riding equipment. It is now on display at the excellent Viking Ship Museum in Oslo.

ZOMBIES

What is the meaning of this vandalization? Historians have argued that there could be many motives at play here, including revenge, punishment and trophy-hunting, or even 'neutralization of the dead'. By removing the grave goods and literally breaking the bones of the deceased, the intruders were making sure that they were unable to interfere with the living – and certainly would not be able to come after the grave robbers for pilfering their valuables.

Grave goods and burial practices in the Viking Age were an important way of creating an identity for the dead. By purposely altering the material remnants of the deceased and their grave goods, perpetrators of these violent acts tampered with their identities and memories. In several saga stories, moreover, mounds were entered by intruders with the purpose of making sure the dead stayed dead.

In *Grettis saga*, the hero Grettir enters the tomb of Kar the Old to confront and kill his animated corpse (*draugr* in Old Norse), which has been terrifying the local neighbourhood. After a struggle, Grettir manages to overcome his foe, cuts off his head and departs, taking the grave goods with him. And there is even physical evidence of this practice. Archaeologists have discovered spears and swords thrust into skeletons, presumably to prevent them walking again.

PUBLIC SPECTACLES

In many cases, the breaking into of graves was not a quick smash-and-grab process. Historians have speculated that it would have taken several days to break into the mound, find the right section, remove or destroy body parts or grave goods, and then reseal the mound as before. Interpretations have therefore viewed it not as an act undertaken at the dead of night, in secret, but rather in full public view – and that, it has been argued, was the whole point.

In the cases of the Oseberg and Gokstad ships in Norway, scholars have estimated that the mound-breakings took place in the second half of the tenth century, which would coincide with the Danish king Harald Bluetooth's efforts to extend control into western Norway. The grand scale of the break-ins of these tombs fits with known attempts by Harald to assert his own hereditary claims, such as the building of the Jelling burial site to entomb his parents, and the ring fortress at Trelleborg. He was seeking to establish his own dynastic and hereditary symbols, while also destroying those of his enemies.

Trelleborg

An immense circular fortress built by Harald Bluetooth near Slagelse in west Zealand, Denmark, as part of his extension of military power. It has been dated using dendrochronology on the timber used for construction to between August 980 and May 981. Only seven such fortresses have been discovered, and Trelleborg is the best preserved. As many as 1,300 people may have lived inside the fortress.

Thus breaking into the grave of an enemy could be a highly public spectacle of violence that the perpetrators *wanted* people to see. They wanted them to see the raiding of grave goods, the new ownership of powerful weaponry, the parading and smashing of the remains of the dead. These were large-scale acts of dominance, a violent demonstration of power by new leaders who wished to attack and supplant the hereditary claims of their rivals.

·8·

COLOUR

Viking-style Norman ships depicted in the Bayeux Tapestry, eleventh century

Colour in the Viking world was a code...

THE VIKING PALETTE

By studying literary texts alongside archaeology, not only are we able to reconstruct the colours as Vikings would have seen them, but we can also begin to understand the different meanings of colours and how they were produced and used by the Vikings.

Lichen from coastal cliffs gave them purples, reds, pinks and violets; the madder plant gave them reds; woad and indigo gave them blues; and a deep orange-yellow was produced from the mineral orpiment. We even know what the Vikings called their eight basic colours, from mentions in Old Norse texts:

blár – blue   *brúnn* – brown
grár – grey   *grœnn* – green
gulr – yellow   *hvítr* – white
rauðr –red   *svartr* – black

The colours known and used by the Vikings were a manifestation of their own history, both at home and abroad. On the one hand they were an expression of their knowledge and understanding of their own Scandinavian environment – knowledge passed down through the centuries – because they extracted colours from roots, plants and insects; on the other, they were intricately linked with the history of trade networks and the expansion of the Viking world, because they also imported dyes from central Asia and the Near East.

SEEING VIKING COLOURS

Such knowledge of their colours is one thing – but what if you could actually *see* a Viking colour as they saw it? Some Viking colours, in fact, have come and gone in our modern world, brief visitors to a place in which they did not belong. In 1904–5, the Oseberg ship burial was excavated in Norway, and inside the mound archaeologists discovered textiles of the most stunning hues, but they soon faded once exposed to the light and air – a powerful reminder that, in archaeology, discovery can often mean destruction. Colours in other artefacts, however, have not faded, and most impressive are the tens of thousands of decorative beads – remains of necklaces worn as personal ornaments – that have been discovered in Viking settlements across Europe.

Not only do Viking beads survive in immense quantity and quality, but also in stunning variety. Most are made of glass, rock crystal (a type of quartz), carnelian (a mineral) and amber (fossilized tree resin), and they display a wide range of designs and crafts – some are decorated, others not; some have gold or silver foil, and others are multicoloured. They also come in all sorts of shapes, from melon-shaped balls to rings, barrels and cylinders.

Importantly, the location and dates of such finds suggest that this riot of colour was new in the Viking Age. Beads that predate the period are predominantly single-colour – either red-brown or orange. But from the mid-600s there is evidence of more advanced colour-making, with beads of white, green and blue becoming prominent. Because of this change from blandness to technicolour, the colourfulness of beads was an indicator of being a Viking.

A COLOUR CODE

One of the most impressive assemblages of beads comes from the Viking trading town of Hedeby, where more than 7,700 beads have been discovered in a variety of locations. These include 400 from graves, over 900 from the harbour, and roughly 6,400 from around the trading settlement itself. Of those in the harbour, 598 beads – mostly blue, green, black and white – were unearthed bunched tightly with seven silver coins, which allowed archaeologists to date the find. The beads are believed to be the contents of a textile or leather purse, lost at some point around the 830s. The purse itself has long since rotted away, leaving the beads in a little pile.

Hedeby

One of the most important Viking archaeological sites so far discovered, Hedeby was a trading town in the south of the Jutland peninsula of Denmark – through which ran the trade routes between the Frankish empire (Francia) and Scandinavia. The town was founded in c. 804, and was destroyed by a Slavic army in 1066.

The 400 beads found in the graves at Hedeby have helped us to understand that, for the Viking inhabitants, certain varieties of colour and material were particularly associated with burial. Similar hues of red, blue and green – as well as a wider variety of yellows and oranges – were discovered, and all of them were made from carnelian or rock crystal rather than glass.

Beads of different colours have also been discovered at different levels of the site – thus reflecting separate periods of occupation – showing that the predominant colours of Viking beads changed over time, as fashions came and went in cycles lasting between ten and thirty-five years. This raises the interesting idea that the Vikings would have identified certain types of bead colour as 'old-fashioned', in terms of being indicative of a period in the past. It is evidence that, to the Vikings, colour itself was an indicator of time passing.

COLOURFUL BUILDINGS

Our understanding of Viking colour also comes from recent work on traces of Viking paint discovered on the remains of buildings. Very few objects have actually been discovered with original Viking colours on them, but archaeologists are now able to reconstruct different shades from remains that are invisible to the naked eye.

Stave church

A type of timber-framed Christian church common in north-western Europe during the Middle Ages. It has been estimated that there were once as many as 1,000 stave churches in Norway alone. They were integral to the changing landscape of Scandinavia during the Viking world's slow conversion to Christianity.

One such artefact is a carved oak plank, once part of a stave church, that was discovered in Hørning in Denmark. Dendro-chronology has dated this plank to a tree that was probably felled between 1060 and 1070, and that was then painted with a floral frieze on one side and a snake motif on the other. The paint was made of linseed oil, in strong colours of red, yellow and black. Most importantly, analysis of the colours has shown that they were made from minerals not found in Denmark. The orpiment used to make the yellow is found in Germany and Turkey; the cinnabar used to make the red comes from Spain. The use of such colours was a demonstration of wealth and of international contacts.

Archaeological studies of this nature make it possible to reconstruct the colourscape of the built environment of Viking Age settlements. Some feasting halls, for example, are believed to have been painted white, as traces of clay and white chalk have been found in excavations at halls in both Tissø and Lejre in Denmark, suggesting that the structures were covered in quicklime. This would have made the halls visible from a long distance, as well as providing better light conditions inside.

Such scientific pigment analysis has allowed chemists and archaeologists from the National Museum of Denmark to create a palette of twelve colours that, based on the limited evidence available, may have been used to decorate buildings in the Viking Age. This has shown that the Vikings liked simple, pure colours: if they painted something, they did it to be noticed. Colours were not mixed with white to lighten them or black to darken them (as became common during the Renaissance) – nor was it possible to mix colours to make others before 1900, because of impurities in the pigments. In the Viking Age, a mixture of colours simply produced a grey colour.

STRIPES

With so much colour in their houses and jewellery, it is perhaps not surprising that the Vikings also embraced colour on their ships. The historical and archaeological evidence is limited but intriguing. Fragments of both white and red woollen cloth from the Gokstad ship burial – perhaps sailcloth – suggest that the sail may have been white with red stripes, possibly organized in vertical lines. And there is reason to believe that this is only one such example. We know from *Heimskringla* that, in 1028, King Cnut attacked Norway with 1,400 ships, which were a spectacular sight.

> When Canute the Mighty had fitted out his army, he had a great crowd of men and very big ships. He himself had a Dragon which was so big that it counted sixty benches and

on it were gold-decked heads. Hacon the Jarl had another Dragon on which there were forty benches, and on it too there were gilded heads. The sails of both were striped with blue and red and green. The ships were all painted above the water...

Heimskringla

A collection of sagas written by Snorri Sturluson, and one of the most important surviving historical accounts of the Viking Age. The book is about the lives of the kings of Sweden and Norway, beginning with their mythical descent from Odin and continuing until 1177. It is based on the works of the early court poets.

This vision of striped sails is supported by the Bayeux Tapestry, the embroidery of which depicts in intricate detail the Norman invasion of England in 1066. The structure and design of the ships and their rigging have a clear Viking ancestry (just like William the Conqueror himself), and some – but not all – are shown with coloured and striped sails.

The belief that Viking sails were striped is also supported by our understanding of the looms that were used to make the linen and wool for the sailcloth. The only way to make large areas of textile in the period (such as those required for a sail) was to weave strips, limited in width by the loom on which they were made, and then sew them together – a perfect reason for making sails with vertical stripes.

·9·
TOYS

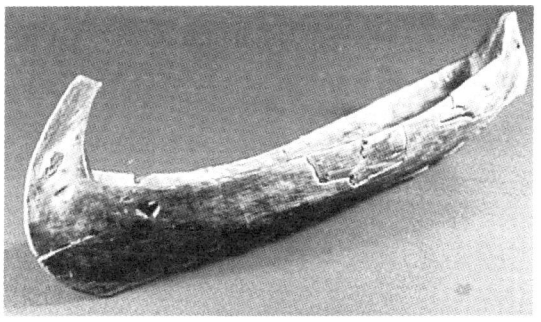

Model toy ship discovered at Winetavern Street in Dublin

Viking toys are all about
hidden children...

Scandinavian babies, toddlers, infants and even teenagers are almost entirely hidden from the historical record of the Viking Age. Reconstructing the history of these invisible Viking children is therefore an exercise in the use of the historical imagination. Children are hidden in the silences and gaps in the records, and an invaluable source for discovering them is toys.

WHERE TO FIND TOYS?

One of the reasons that Viking children are hidden from history is that very few records survive that shed light on their world. They are underrepresented in the archaeological evidence of burials; no rune stones were inscribed in their memory as they were with other social groups; and they are mentioned only fleetingly in the sagas.

One of the very rare literary references to children playing with toys comes from a passage in *Víga-Glúms saga*, which describes one child passing a small bronze horse to another to play with. More typically, however, children are simply described as being 'at play'. In the saga *Bolla þáttr Bollasonar*, Þorðr's son Óláfr is described as 'then seven or eight winters old. He went from the farm to play and build himself a house, as it is customary for children to do.'

Víga-Glúms saga

This thirteenth-century Icelandic saga recounts the life of Glúmr Eyjólfsson, a powerful and bloodthirsty man who commits numerous murders but attempts to cover up his guilt. It is set in northern Iceland in the environs of Eyjafjörður. It is particularly interesting to historians for its treatment of both pagan and Christian beliefs and customs, and Glúmr's conversion at the end of his life.

Such examples may be colourful, but there are too few for historians to grapple with, and so it is in the discovery of small objects – usually interpreted as children's toys – that we can begin to get a better look at hidden Viking children.

Miniature artefacts have been discovered at settlement sites and in cemeteries containing children's graves, such as Birka in Sweden and Barshalder in Gotland. The scarcity of child graves suggests that infants may have been buried away from adults, or in a manner that is hard to discern today. Some historians have conjectured that the small number of children's graves may have been contributed to by infanticide, with unmarried mothers presumably disposing of the corpses of unwanted babies covertly in order to avoid public disapproval.

In those graves known to be associated with children, various objects considered as toys have been found, including small bronze rattles or bells. A hexagonal copper bell, for example, was excavated from a ninth- or tenth-century grave connected with a child at Peel Castle on the Isle of Man. This particular bell has been viewed as a plaything of a child from a wealthy family.

Other examples of Viking toys include musical instruments known as 'buzz-discs' – discs with two holes drilled through which whirred when pulled on a thread – as well as string rattles, beads, carved ships, wooden swords, dolls, model horses and other animal figures. The small items that have survived are generally made of bone, wood or sometimes metal.

The history of children does not simply rely on toys for which there is material evidence, however. It is also likely that children invented their own toys. A simple wooden spoon could become an oar, a sword, a wand or even a doll. Children may have played with pebbles, beads, wood, bones, clay pots or other organic materials found in or near the household. We know they played with balls – and in winter presumably they threw snowballs, something that is hinted at in the tale of a twelfth-century nobleman in Nidaros (medieval Trondheim). To his cost, he mistook the whizz of an axe for the sound of a child throwing a snowball.

BOYS' TOYS?

A number of objects traditionally seen as 'boys' toys' have been discovered during excavations in Dublin and Trondheim, among other places, including miniature wooden horses, swords, boats, weapons and tools. Traditionally archaeologists have viewed these small items as belonging to children, though there are intriguing questions about ownership that still remain unanswered, since small figures and weapons may also have had a votive or ritual function for adults. An intricately carved wooden horse found at Trondheim and dating from 1100–1125 has typically been viewed as a child's toy, but the attention paid by the carver to its sexual organ also suggests an alternative, perhaps adult, use.

The division between miniature adult objects and children's toys is sometimes a blurred one. There is evidence, for example, of children being buried with small axes or tools, as well as small querns (hand mills) or stones intended for grinding. Scaled-down versions of adult objects were one of the ways in which Viking children were socialized and taught the trades and techniques they would encounter in the Viking Age economy.

In the same way, it is believed that the existence of wooden toy boats is connected to teaching children about the art of seafaring, something that is reinforced by evidence found in the sagas. *Króka-Refs saga*, for example, describes a 'Norwegian's son [who] had for a plaything a ship', a toy he had brought with him from Norway at the end of the tenth or beginning of the eleventh century.

These literary echoes of childish behaviour are mirrored in what survives in the material record. Excavations of Viking Dublin around Winetavern Street and Fishamble Street uncovered five model ships dating from the tenth century to the thirteenth century, the earliest example being a Viking-style boat or ship found in a pit and wrapped in a pillow for protection. Archaeologists also discovered a small wooden sword measuring 23.7 centimetres in length – and other child-sized Viking Age wooden swords have been found elsewhere in Ireland.

Viking Dublin

The Vikings arrived in Dublin during the ninth century, with contemporary annals referring to the building of a *longphort* (shore fortress) by 841. They were expelled in 902 but returned in 917, when they built a more organized town. During the Viking reign, Dublin became the most important town in Ireland and was a hub of westward expansion and trade. It is one of the best-known Viking towns because of the extensive excavations, and the quality and quantity of the material discovered.

Our interest in these toys is not simply limited to an interest in who owned them, but also in what children actually did with them and why. How did they spend their free time, and how far can we reconstruct the culture of Viking childhood? Typically, miniature martial objects are thought to have instilled in young boys something of the masculine adult culture found in the sagas. In other words, in playing with toy boats and wielding small-sized swords, Viking children were playing at adult forms of behaviour – helping to transition them into adult Viking society.

HIDDEN GIRLS

The reconstruction of the lives of Viking girls from the evidence of the toys with which they played is even more difficult, as they are doubly invisible: they are hidden from the historic record that survives, and past historians were not conditioned to even look for them in the first place. We have seen that there are literary sources that refer to girls engaging in imaginary role-playing with boys, though of the three children described in *Brennu-Njáls saga*, the girl appears to have assumed the role of property:

> One of the boys said, I'll be Mord and summon you to give up your wife for not having sex with her. The other boy answered, I'll be Hrut, and I say that you must forfeit all property claims if you don't dare to fight with me.

Presumably these boys were fighting over the girl, whose character was being viewed in sexual terms.

It is perhaps artificial to distinguish rigidly between toys used by girls and those used by boys, however. Among young children at least, it is highly likely that many toys were played with by children of either sex. Nonetheless, if we view toys as part of the socialization of Viking children, it is probable that – in their strictly hierarchical and patriarchal society – there existed female equivalents of boys' toys which taught girls how to grow up to be Viking women.

A number of miniature carvings of the human form survive, perhaps indicative that dolls were played with by young girls. Such dolls were often simply carved as crude cut-outs, but others have facial features and later examples sometimes have carved clothes. From these strands of material evidence, one can conjecture that girls were being taught to assume the roles of wives and mothers through such toys.

One of the most important discoveries relating to Viking girls is the excavation of the grave of a five- or six-year-old girl in Birka in Sweden. Contained in the burial site near the skeleton were a number of objects buried as grave goods, including a small knife, a needle case made of bone, a round gilded copper brooch, and a number of blue, yellow and gold- and silver-foil glass beads. The beads themselves were perhaps playthings, while the needle case may indicate that young girls were taught to sew as part of assuming a domestic role within Viking society.

Of course, the difficulty with Viking 'toys' is that it's hard to know whether they were even intended for children in the first place. They may have been primarily used by adults, in which case those Viking children slip away, once more hidden from history.

·10·
TEETH

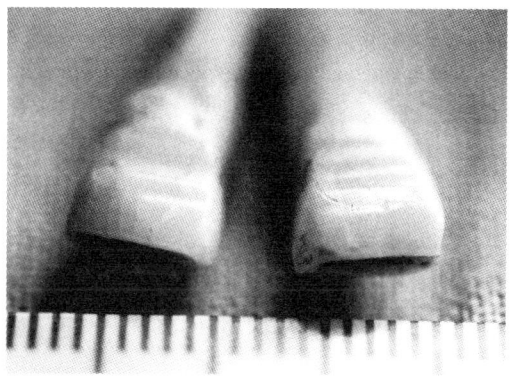

Filed teeth found among Viking remains in a burial pit
uncovered in Dorset, UK

Teeth are all about Viking identity...

Viking teeth are an unexpectedly rich source of information, telling us much about behaviour, social status and ethnicity. The archaeological survival of teeth is not a matter of happenstance; they are made of enamel – the hardest substance in the human body. While the degree of wear on Viking gnashers is a useful index of diet and general dental hygiene, much more surprising perhaps is the evidence of deliberate dental modification in an age long before the modern-day craze for the bling of gold caps and diamond-inlaid teeth.

MARKS OF FEROCITY?

One of the most remarkable archaeological studies in recent years has revealed the Viking practice of deliberately filing horizontal grooves into the crown of the incisors at the front of the mouth. A study looking at some 557 skeletons of Viking men, women and children by a Swedish archaeologist revealed that, of this number, 24 skeletons – all male – had teeth that were marked in this manner. The skeletons sampled were from across Scandinavia, from Viking Age cemeteries in Fjälkinge, Trelleborg and Öland in Sweden, as well as in Denmark.

This was not the result of overenthusiastic teeth-cleaning with a stick, which might cause some degree of wear, but rather intentional and skilled work by someone practised in the art of tooth-filing. In most cases the furrows were horizontal and shallow, with some in the shape of a half-moon or orange segment. In a small number of instances, the grooves filed were much more pronounced – up to 2.5 millimetres deep – which undoubtedly would have been in danger of going through the enamel and into the dentine and soft pulp beneath. An experiment on an ancient tooth using a metal file – similar to one excavated as part of the Mästermyr find in Sweden – revealed that this was a process that would take twenty minutes or more of fairly constant work, something that modern-day dentists argue would certainly have been uncomfortable, if not painful in its more extreme forms.

The Mästermyr find

One of the most remarkable discoveries to shed light on Viking Age metalwork is a mid-ninth-century blacksmith's toolbox found in Mästermyr mire on the island of Gotland, Sweden. Contained in this wooden chest were around 200 metal tools and numerous projects in various stages of completion. It is believed that the chest belonged to a travelling craftsman, and it is now on display in the Swedish History Museum in Stockholm.

What puzzles Viking experts, though, is the reason for these marks. Why did Vikings file their teeth? Such markings are unique among Europeans of the period, and it has been suggested that they were learned from contact with the Americas, since teeth-filing of this sort was practised by the Native American tribes of the Great Lakes region. But perhaps more plausible is that they developed it on their own, and one possible explanation is that it was part of their warrior identity – indeed, some historians have conjectured that they did it to instil a sense of fear in their enemies. There is evidence that at least some of the men with filed teeth in the Swedish study were connected to cultures of violence, as a number of them had decapitated skeletons and battle injuries, from which we might infer that they were warriors.

It has been proposed that Vikings may have bared their teeth in battle, and that colouring the teeth with black or red dyes or pigment might have made the furrows much more visible from a distance as one charged at the enemy. But while there may be some element of truth in these fearsome imaginings, as historians we must beware this kind of sensationalism: warrior identity is only one possible explanation for tooth modification.

INITIATION?

Tempting as it is to see filed teeth as a mark of Viking warriors, it is questionable whether they would in fact have been visible beneath facial hair and lips. Further archaeological studies of teeth modification – in locations such as Birka in eastern-central Sweden or the Viking Age cemetery of Kopparsvik on the island of Gotland – have extended our knowledge of this practice. We know that tooth modification took place from the 750s to the 1100s, and while it was certainly a male-only custom there remains significant scope for various kinds of meanings to have been attached to it.

One of the most striking features of the examples found is the sheer variety of marks that archaeologists have observed – from low-grade superficial abrasions, to multiple horizontal furrows into the enamel, to quite deep lesions into the dentine and pulp. It may be that these differentiations are just symptomatic of natural variations in the teeth themselves or different methods of modifying teeth, but more interesting is the possibility that they relate to different social identities. Many of the skeletons discovered with teeth modifications, for example, were buried in important trading places, including Kopparsvik, Sigtuna, Birka, Trelleborg and Othems. In many cultures, tooth modification is used as a form of initiation rite or induction, and it may be that what we are seeing here is a dental marker identifying a closed group of merchants.

WHO DO YOU THINK YOU ARE?

The science of tooth analysis has further implications for the study of Viking identity, beyond the realm of tooth modification. Indeed, teeth have proved a brilliant way of looking at Viking DNA.

One of the biggest problems with trying to study ancient DNA is the contamination of archaeological sites by the archaeologists and anthropologists themselves. Scientists have discovered that one of the ways around this is to study teeth, which can be clinically removed from the jawbones of skeletons and then tested in what genomic scientists describe as 'clean laboratories'.

Chemical analysis of the teeth recovered at the Ridgeway Hill mass grave site in Dorset was instrumental in identifying the ethnic identities of the more than fifty decapitated skeletons found buried there. It proved that none were from Britain, but rather they were from Arctic and sub-Arctic regions of Norway,

Ridgeway Hill burial pit

A mass grave, in a disused Roman quarry near Weymouth in Dorset, containing fifty-four male skeletons, mainly of young adults, all of whom had been decapitated. Fifty-one heads were found, carefully piled up on one side of the grave. It is believed that these were a band of captured Viking raiders, executed by Anglo-Saxons. Radiocarbon dating places the burial in the period 970–1025 CE.

Sweden, Iceland, Belarus and Russia. In a similar way, the age of the young girl buried in a grave at Birka (see p. 75) was deduced from her dental records. Teeth are therefore uniquely able to uncover aspects of the true identity of Viking Age Scandinavians.

·11·
DOORS

The Gotland image stone depicting a woman
standing at the threshold of a door

Viking doors are all about death…

Writing the history of Viking doors is difficult, because so few actual examples survive. What remain instead are the frames that would have supported them, as well as furniture such as rings and hinges. There are also depictions of doors, such as those on the Gotland picture stones, and they feature prominently in literary sources. Intriguingly, one of the things we know from this combination of evidence is that Viking doors were intimately linked to Viking death.

Gotland picture stones

The Gotland picture stones are decorated slabs of stone which date from 400-1100, found on the Baltic island of Gotland, Sweden. Over 400 examples survive and they depict images of myth and legends, sometimes combined with runes. The stones are shaped as doors, and are placed at border points on the landscape; they have a strong symbolic meaning as 'doors' between the living and the dead.

Doors functioned as thresholds or boundaries that needed to be controlled. They were liminal spaces – most obviously between the inside of the household and the outside world, but also between the earthly and the supernatural, the living and the dead. As portals from one realm to another, doors were objects of great significance and causes of social anxiety.

DOORS TO THE DEAD

An important example of the symbolic importance of doors in Viking funerary practices comes from the eyewitness account of the Arabic diplomat and traveller Ahmad ibn Fadlan, who described a Viking ship burial on the Volga River in 922. The ritual involved the burial of a powerful chieftain, and the rape, sacrifice and burial of one of his female slaves.

Ibn Fadlan described how the girl was forced to have intercourse with the dead warrior's men, before being led outside to a construction 'which looked like the frame of a door'. She was then passed over the door three times in a ritual where she 'met' the dead: first her mother and father, then another dead relative, and finally her dead master. This door thus assumed a role of connecting the living with the dead. Next, she was laid beside her master on the ship and tied up, before a woman known as 'the Angel of Death' repeatedly plunged a knife between her ribs as men pulled on a rope around her neck. The boat was then burned.

In the Viking world, doors were also locations in which one could actually communicate with the dead, who were seen to possess special powers and secret knowledge that could be passed on to the living. Walking through or standing inside ritualized doors like the one that marked the entrance to a funerary ship, or the passageway to a burial mound, allowed people to gain this knowledge. Thus, in the thirteenth-century poem *Hevararkviða*, or *The Waking of Angantyr*, a daughter stands at the doorway of the burial mound of her dead father and brothers, seeking permission to obtain a famous sword interred with them, which she needs to avenge their deaths. And the poem *Grógaldr* speaks of a son waking his dead sorceress mother with 'Wake thee, Groa, Wake, mother good, At the doors of the dead I call thee'.

BURIAL IN DOORWAYS

Another mortuary practice found in the Viking Age was that of burying people either in doorways or under the threshold of a door. In *Laxdæla saga* the figure Hrapp calls his wife during an illness, fearing that it will 'put an end to our life together', and asks of her:

> Now, when I am dead, I wish my grave to be dug in the doorway of my fire hall, and that I be put thereinto, standing there in the doorway; then I shall be able to keep a more searching eye on my dwelling.

Burial under the threshold allowed the dead to keep watch over what was going on among the living.

It appears that doorway burials did occur in practice. Archaeological analysis of longhouses in south-western Norway has yielded several sites at which this was carried out, including a dwelling in Ullandhaug where a concentration of forty-two iron nails has been interpreted as the remains of a casket set inside a doorway. Alongside the nails were burnt human bone and an axe which archaeologists have dated to the ninth century.

One of the most extraordinary examples of this kind of doorway burial was that of the 'Elk-man', discovered in 1988 at Birka in Sweden. Here, two male bodies were buried on top of each other under the threshold of a doorway. On top, placed in a hunched position, was a large man in his twenties who had been decapitated, his head placed at the level of his chest. Below him was a warrior aged between forty and fifty, buried face up, with weaponry, beads, and a set of elk antlers by his head. The significance of the antlers may be connected to a belief in the transformation in death from human to animal.

In each of these cases, doors were central to the ritual of Viking funerals as well as to the journey of the deceased from the living world to that of the dead. They were viewed as an access point to other realms, but this meant that such barriers also had to be controlled – to prevent the dead from entering the world of the living.

One mortuary practice thought to be an ancient tradition is that of the corpse door or cadaver door. It features in the saga literature, as well as surviving as an architectural feature in ancient houses.

After relatives closed the eyes, mouth and nostrils of the deceased – an act of figuratively closing the cadaver's 'doorways' – a hole was made in the external wall to create the corpse door. This was done either by removing bricks or stones from the wall, or by cutting a hole in wooden planks. A reconstructed example of a corpse door, cut out of a wooden wall and then sealed, can be seen in the open-air museum at Nordfjord, Norway.

Once this exit was made, the body was passed outside through the hole instead of being carried through the main door. The corpse door was then resealed before the funeral party returned home, the idea being that the ghost of the departed would be unable to find its way back again, since the exit no longer existed. In this manner, the boundaries of the house were maintained and the dead were barred from the house.

A variation on this theme is the phenomenon of the Viking 'door court'. Here, the door acted as a symbolic court at which the dead were judged. One of the clearest examples of the use of a door court is found in *Eyrbyggja saga*, which tells of an Icelandic farm suffering repeated attacks from the living dead. In response to this, the farmer calls all the dead to assemble at the main door of the farm. He then proceeds to put them all on trial, and one by one they are all vanquished and expelled from the farm.

·12·
GOADING

Gunnhild provokes her sons to take revenge, nineteenth-century illustration.
Gunnhild was the wife of Erik Bloodaxe. She appears in several sagas
including *Fagrskinna, Egils saga, Njáls saga* and *Heimskringla*

Viking goading is all about challenging
male authority...

Feuding was an important part of Viking life, and within those feuds women played an important role as inciters of violence. They did this by goading – wielding words as weapons – with the aim of annoying or provoking an assailant to action. In mobilizing taunts against their target's insecurities, the aim was to challenge a man's masculinity by piercing his sense of honour and self-worth. Goading allowed Viking women significant – although unofficial – power, in which their words were equivalent to men's deeds.

A TAUNTING WIFE

A fine example of women admonishing men verbally comes from *Laxdæla saga*, in which Guðrún winds up her husband, Bolli Þorleiksson, to take revenge on Kjartan, his foster brother and close friend, who has scorned and rejected her. 'With your temperament,' she begins, criticizing her husband's inaction:

> you'd have made some farmer a good group of daughters, fit to do no one any good or any harm. After all the abuse and shame Kjartan has heaped upon you, you don't let it disturb your sleep while he goes riding by under your very nose, with only one other man to accompany him. Such men have no better memory than a pig. There's not much chance you'll ever dare to make a move against Kjartan at home if you won't even stand up to him now, when he only has one or two others to back him up. The lot of you just sit here at home, making much of yourselves, and one could only wish there were fewer of you.

Guðrún then goes on, threatening to end their marriage if Bolli does not kill Kjartan. This type of threat, pivoting on sexual or financial sanctions, was common in the sagas. They are full of threats such as 'you shall never come in my bed again' or 'I shall let my father repossess my property'.

In this case, Guðrún's ultimatum was quite the speech – and it worked. Kjartan was ambushed by Bolli and Guðrún's brothers, and although Bolli was reluctant to take part in the attack he was the one who finally struck Kjartan down with his sword, fatally wounding him, though he instantly regretted it.

TAUNTING MOTHERS

Bolli's regret, however, is not enough for Kjartan's mother, who in turn incites the rest of her sons to the murder of Bolli in another fabulous example of Viking invective:

> Marvellously unlike your noble kindred you turn out in that you will not avenge such a brother as Kjartan was; never would Egil, your mother's father, have behaved in such a manner; and a piteous thing it is to have dolts for sons; indeed, I think it would have suited you better if you had been your father's daughter and had married. For here, Halldor, it comes to the old saw: 'No stock without a duffer', and this is the ill-luck of Olaf I see most clearly, how he blundered in begetting his sons.

Shortly afterwards the boys form an armed pack, including Kjartan's mother, to hunt Bolli down, and when they find him with Guðrún they chop off his head.

The image of mothers taunting sons is relatively common in Icelandic sagas, and is played out in *Kjalnesinga saga*. The over-bearing mother Þorgerðr has grown weary of her son, Kolfinnur, who spends his days in a mood, loafing at home 'stretching out his long legs'. She urges him to go to the nearby farm where she knows men are playing board games, and two suitors are vying for the hand of a woman named Ólöf the Fair.

Kjalnesinga saga

One of the latest Icelandic sagas, dating from around 1300. It tells the story of the people who lived in Kjalarnes, an area underneath Mount Esja, across the bay from modern Reykjavík. It is particularly valuable for its consideration of outlaws in Viking society, the paranormal, and beliefs and culture in Viking Age Ireland – the hero, Búi, is of Irish descent and lives with his Irish foster mother.

Þorgerðr wants her son up and out, taking his future in his hands. Fed up, she delivers a stinging verbal reprimand: 'You're so sluggish that you just lie by the firepit, a distress to your mother. It would be better that you were dead than to know of such disgrace in your family.' Suitably chastised, Kolfinnur gets up, goes to the farm and meets Ólöf. He subsequently kills one of the suitors and fights a duel with the other.

What is most interesting here is the way that female family figures – a wife and a mother – are able to utilize goading in order to humiliate their menfolk into action. The strength and effectiveness of the criticisms lie in the ways in which these women challenge the masculinity and honour of their male relatives through emotional language.

VIKING MISOGYNY

Such depictions of female goading in the Viking world must be handled by historians with great care. Read one way, they appear to offer representations of women taking power into their own hands as a way of challenging male authority. But it is important to note that the sagas were written and commissioned by men, and the narratives they contain shift the blame for violence away from the man to the goading woman. In some cases, the woman becomes the scapegoat for the man's misdeed.

These tales were also a warning for their male audience: what happens if the power of such women is not controlled? The result is made clear – chaos and violence. Buried in these narratives, therefore, is a misogynistic Viking fear of women in positions of power and authority, which played on male anxieties.

PROVOKING WARRIORS

The evidence suggests that this taunting was not just one-way, a line of electricity running only from provocative women to bullied men. Men were also happy to taunt each other. The sagas are full of such teases: a Viking warrior at a horse fight mocked for his 'little blonde beard'; a Viking youngster, described as a 'cesspool-hog' and ridiculed for his 'downy-cheeks'. Such jibes aimed to emasculate an opponent.

Goading was also an important part of battle. In *Þórðar saga hreðu*, the main protagonist Þórður is caught by his enemy Össur while he is visiting his horse at his favourite grazing spot. He is attacked by six of Össur's men, but his defence is so impressive that not one of them is able to wound him. When the attack abates, Þórður points out to Össur that, if their positions were swapped, 'I should not wish to be called these men's foreman, and use them only as a shield' – essentially teasing him for

Þórðar saga hreðu

Late-fourteenth-century Icelandic saga concerning Þórður Þórðarson, or Thord the Menace, a carpenter, poet and warrior. The saga is particularly useful for its depiction of honour, marriage, revenge and reconciliation. It is full of dramatic battles and ambushes.

hiding behind them. He then goads Össur into launching an attack himself.

The taunt works, and enrages Össur so much that he unleashes an uncontrolled lunge at his foe, which Þórður neatly blocks with his shield. He then cuts Össur so deeply in the chest that his ribs are separated from his spine, unsurprisingly killing him.

Historians believe that a Viking taunt was also central to the outcome of the Battle of Maldon, fought between Anglo-Saxon forces and Danish raiders on the banks of the River Blackwater in Essex on 11 August 991, during one of the most significant Viking campaigns of the period. The Vikings won a famous and important victory, which led to the first payment of Danegeld by the Anglo-Saxons. Essentially, this was a bribe to make the Vikings go home – in this case 3,300 kilograms of silver, the weight of two family cars.

A narrative of the battle survives in an eponymous poem written down in the late eleventh century. A key moment in the battle occurred early on when the Anglo-Saxon leader, Byrht-noth, gave ground and allowed the Vikings to cross a narrow and easily defensible causeway running from a small island to the mainland. It was a fundamental, obvious and easily avoidable error that directly led to the defeat, and Byrhtnoth's motivation has foxed scholars for generations.

It has been argued that his actions were a direct response to a personal or perhaps religious taunt directed at him from the Viking leader, Olaf. The details, however, remain teasingly beyond our grasp, and what survives is nothing more than a sense that the Vikings acted somehow treacherously to the Anglo-Saxon mind recording the battle, who almost spits out the line 'Then the hateful visitors began to use guile'.

The details of this most successful taunt for now remain hidden in the meaning of the Anglo-Saxon words *ofermod* (meaning 'pride') and *lytegian* (meaning 'dissimulation' and 'craftiness'), which appear in the poem. It's nonetheless clear that, in this way, Viking taunting could profoundly influence the making of the Viking world.

·13·

CRIMINAL
PROFILING

Egill Skallagrímsson in a seventeenth-century
manuscript of *Egil's saga*

*Criminal profiling is all about
Viking appearance...*

A TENDENCY TO VIOLENCE

The Vikings were interested in the relationship between appearance and behaviour, and were concerned in particular with the appearance of violent men. Evidence for this comes from the Icelandic sagas, in which violent, risk-taking, anti-social men – such as outlaws, murderers and warriors – tended to share certain physical characteristics.

A good example comes from the early-thirteenth-century *Egil's saga*. When we first meet Egill Skallagrímsson, our roguish protagonist, the saga's author wallows in his appearance:

> Egil had very distinctive features, with a wide forehead... [his] beard grew over a long, broad part of his face and his chin and entire jaw were very broad, [he had a] thick neck and broad shoulders... [was] prematurely bald... [and had] a harsh looking face.

Egil's saga

An Icelandic saga chronicling the lives of Egill Skallagrímsson (c.910–c.990), a warrior, farmer and poet, and his family. The work is anonymous, but some historians believe that it was written by Snorri Sturluson (see p. 32). Egil's life is both bewildering and extraordinary, and the text provides the most vivid details of Viking feuds, fights, love, magic, cruelty and mourning.

Egill committed his first murder at the age of seven, cleaving in two the skull of a child who cheated in a game. His subsequent life was littered with blood feuds and a string of further murders. He became wealthy through farming, politics and war, and just before his own death he buried his silver with the help of two servants – who, of course, he then murdered in order to keep the hoard's location safe.

Another example of criminal profiling comes from *Laxdœla saga*, in which a shepherd boy is chased and attacked by a group of ruffians. They included Þorgils Holluson, a 'large man of manly build, balding between the temples', and Bolli Bollason, who had a 'wide forehead and full cheeks' and was 'well built at the shoulders and broad under the arms'. And in *Göngu-Hrólfs saga*, Atli – an outlaw, murderer and robber – is described as being 'of large build... thick-browed and heavily bearded'.

Recent research has demonstrated that, when they appear in the sagas, these types of violent, criminally minded men have at least one of the following traits: large and bushy beards, thick eyebrows, a prominent brow and chin, a broad face, a large chest in relation to the waist, baldness and developed musculature – all of which are now known to be physical signs of high testosterone levels.

But it was not just a thuggish physique that gave criminals away for the saga writers; it was also their eyes. The eyes were seen as a window into unsavoury personalities, and were believed to show malicious intent. Although there are plenty of examples of characters being 'bright-eyed' or 'happy-eyed', in *Brennu-Njáls saga* the beautiful but dangerous maiden Hallgerður Hoskuldsdóttir is described as having 'thief's eyes'; and various sagas include characters who are 'fierce-eyed', 'darting-eyed' or 'sour-eyed'.

A PHYSIOGNOMY

It has been argued that the similar and repeated descriptions in the thirteenth-century sagas reflect knowledge as it stood in the eighth to tenth centuries, and that they were part of an established way of assessing character and personalities by observing physical appearance. This was a Scandinavian version of an ancient European science known as 'physiognomy'.

The existence of this method of assessment in the Viking Age, hinted at in the sagas, is supported by a treatise on physiognomy in Old Norse, which survives in Iceland in two manuscripts, one dating from 1473 and another from c.1500. Both are a type of encyclopedia or miscellany, and are clearly based on the ideas of the Greek sophist Marcus Antonius Polemon (c.88–144), the father of the science of physiognomy. Historians think it likely that Polemon's ideas would have been known in Scandinavia in their original Latin form (Latin was introduced to Scandinavia with Christianity) suggesting that knowledge of his work predates the actual Old Norse translation.

THE LEGAL SYSTEM

The Viking legal system, however, was rather more sophisticated, and required far more than someone being untrustworthy- or ferocious-looking to judge them as guilty. The Vikings had a legislative assembly, known as the Þing (the 'Althing'), which met in specific locations at regular times, and acted as a mechanism to avoid feuds and social unrest. It was presided over by elected chieftains or kings, and was where legal cases were brought in front of a 'law-sayer' or lawspeaker – a man who could recite the unwritten laws and codes that formed their oral legal culture. The presumed facts of the case were then established to determine the accused's innocence or guilt. In theory, this happened on a 'one person, one vote' basis, but in reality it was the most powerful in the community who dominated. If found guilty, the accused would be sentenced to a fine or made an outlaw.

Viking outlaws

Outlawry for the Vikings was the most severe form of punishment. An outlaw was banished by society and would receive no legal or social protection. The outlaw's property was confiscated, and they could receive no food, support or help from anyone, on threat of outlawry themselves. They could also be killed by anyone, without retribution. An unusual aspect of outlawry in Iceland was that the outlaw was not allowed to be transported from the island, essentially turning Iceland itself into a prison.

Viking behaviour – in theory at least – was therefore bound by reasonably sophisticated rules and honour codes, but in practice, in an age that was defined by aggressive competition for land and resources, transgressing those rules was by no means unusual. Viking raids on foreign countries are well known, but less so are the social problems at home caused by this warrior-culture: to survive in the Viking Age, you needed to be able to see danger coming.

BLUSHING

If you were the criminal in question and had been caught and found guilty, it is unlikely that you would have blushed with shame. In the pre-Christian period as depicted by the sagas, turning red with shame was an alien concept in Viking pagan warrior-culture, though a man whose face flushed was very likely to be a threat. They had a word for this physical reaction showing intense anger: the verb *roðna*, meaning 'to go red, to flush'.

A fine example, and one of many in the sagas, comes from *Orkneyinga saga* (c.1300), when Earl Páll discovers that relics of St Magnus are to be brought to Kirkwall in Orkney. Magnus, Earl of Orkney from 1106, had been murdered on Egilsay, another of the Orkney Islands, in 1116, and was initially buried where he fell. His body was then moved to Birsay, before his nephew laid claim to Orkney and moved Magnus once more, this time to Kirkwall on mainland Orkney. Earl Páll fiercely objected to the proposed move, and the saga records that he then 'remained silent as though he had water in his mouth, and turned as red as blood'.

This kind of angry reaction was so common that, in one saga, the author carefully noted its unexpected absence. In *Fóstbrœðra saga* (*The Saga of the Sworn Brothers*), Þorgeirr receives news that his father has been killed, upon which:

> He did not redden, because anger did not run through his skin; he did not turn pale, because he had no hatred in his chest; he did not go livid, because anger did not run through his bones; on the contrary, he did not show any reaction when he was told the news.

Fóstbrœðra saga

The saga, which dates from c.1200, tells the story of two sworn brothers, Þorgeirr and Þormóðr, as they bring quarrelling, chaos and violence to Iceland, Norway and Greenland. It is particularly useful for historians because of its varied portrayals of women.

·14·

BIRDS

A coin of Anlaf Guthfrithsson, King of Jorvik 939–41.
The bird is either a raven or an eagle

Birds are all about Viking myths...

Viking culture fluttered with birds. The evidence of osteoarchae-ology (the study of animal bones from archaeological sites) shows us that birds were a common feature of the Viking diet; we also know that the flight distances of birds were used for navigation, exotic species such as peacocks symbolized foreignness, and birds' feathers were used to stuff pillows. But alongside these practical avian friends were fascinating flocks of mythological birds.

INFORMATION-GATHERERS

Birds communicated with Vikings more than any other animal, and were seen as wise – as nature's purveyors of truth – because they could fly. This unique ability to transcend boundaries between earth and air captured the Viking imagination.

Two of the most famous birds in Norse legend were the pair of ravens, Hugin and Munin, which perched on the shoulders of the god Odin, and flew all over the world gathering information for him. Their knowledge was a source of great power and has clear links to the Viking seafaring tradition: one of the many techniques that the Vikings used to establish their location at sea was to release land-sighting birds, and they favoured ravens. The bird would fly up from the ship's deck and towards any land that it could see, or it would settle back down on the ship if none was visible.

Odin's ravens feature in various Old Norse literary texts – including the *Poetic Edda*, the *Prose Edda*, the *Third Grammatical Treatise* and *Heimskringla* – revealing an interesting picture of these avian information-gatherers. The birds were even given speech by Odin, who was himself referred to as the 'raven-god'. Snorri Sturluson in his *Prose Edda* explained that:

Two ravens sit on Odin's shoulders, and into his ears they tell all the news they see or hear. Their names are Hugin [Thought] and Munin [Mind, Memory]. At sunrise he sends them off to fly throughout the whole world, and they return in time for the first meal. Thus he gathers knowledge about many things that are happening, and so people call him the raven-god.

In the *Poetic Edda* Odin fears that they may not return to him:

Hugin and Munin fly each day
over the spacious earth.
I fear for Hugin, that he come not back,
yet more anxious am I for Munin.

His concern was fully understandable, since these ravens were Odin's eyes and ears in places that he could not be, and therefore in many ways they were the key to his power: it was through them that he learned what was going on in the world. His greater anxiety for Munin may suggest that the birds flew on separate missions, and on this occasion Munin's was the more dangerous. A further clue to Odin's worry about his ravens comes in a passage from the *Third Grammatical Treatise*, which relates that 'Two ravens flew from Hnikar's [Odin's] / shoulders; Huginn to the hanged and / Muninn to the slain', suggesting the hazardous nature of their journeys.

One of the most striking depictions of Odin's ravens comes from Thorwald's Cross, a fragment of a stone cross found on the Isle of Man, possibly carved c.940. It depicts Odin in a battle during the conflict of Ragnarök, which in Viking mythology heralded the end of the world. On one side of the cross he is shown stabbing a wolf with his spear as it consumes him, with one of his ravens sitting on his shoulder.

Through the association with Odin as an information-gatherer – as well as its practical seafaring use – the raven was an important symbol for the Vikings, and the bird featured in designs on armour, shields, helmets, coins and ships.

VALHALLA

Birds – and ravens in particular – are also connected in Viking myth to Valhalla, the majestic hall in the Norse world of Asgard ruled over by Odin, where half of those who died in combat travelled to spend their time in the afterlife, guided there by valkyries, mythical female figures. The remaining half of the dead passed to the goddess Freyja's field, Fólkvangr.

This meant that valkyries would come across ravens in their work, since they were scavengers found on battlefields. In the fragmentary poem *Hrafnsmál* ('Raven song') we are introduced to a conversation between a raven and a valkyrie, as she seeks out the dead to send Valhalla-wards. During their exchange, we learn of the deeds of Harald I of Norway (Harald Fairhair). The valkyrie is depicted as 'high-minded' and 'golden-haired', in contrast to the gore-soaked raven that has been scavenging the dead. The female creature addresses the bird:

> How is it, ye ravens – whence are ye come now
> with beaks all gory, at break of morning?
> Carrion-reek ye carry, and your claws are bloody.
> Were ye near, at night-time, where ye knew of corpses?

The raven shakes himself, and then replies that it is Harald who he has followed 'since out of egg we crept'. The raven is represented as a knowledgeable observer of the battlefield, and is questioned about the exploits of others in the fight, including the Berserkers. It is through the raven's replies that the narrative of the hostilities unfolds.

Birds even lived in Valhalla itself – such as the rooster Gullinkambi, who appears in the famous *Poetic Edda* poem *Völuspá*.

His crowing is foretold to signify the beginning of the events of Ragnarök.

BLOOD EAGLES

In Norse mythology, the eagle was closely associated with blood and death, and the 'blood eagle' has become known as an infamous method of execution that features in Viking sagas. It is usually explained as the torturing of a defeated warrior by splitting open his back and pulling out his lungs and ribs in the manner of a splayed eagle. The legend of the blood eagle is mentioned in two instances in Norse sagas, in reference to the deaths of two noblemen – Prince Hálfdan Haaleg ('Long-leg') and Ælla, King of Northumbria – each killed in retaliation for the murder of a father.

Hálfdan's death is described both in *Orkneyinga saga* (as a sacrifice to Odin), and by the Icelandic poet and historian Snorri Sturluson in his *Heimskringla*. In the latter it is Einarr, one of the earls of Orkney, who performs the deed:

> Afterwards, Earl Einarr went up to Hálfdan and cut the 'blood eagle' on his back, in this fashion that he thrust his sword into his chest by the backbone and severed all the ribs down to the loins, and then pulled out the lungs; and that was Hálfdan's death.

The death of King Ælla is described in a similar vein in the *Tale of Ragnar's Sons*. This saga tells of his capture by Ivar the Boneless in the aftermath of a battle for control over York: 'They caused the bloody eagle to be carved on the back of Ælla, and they cut away all of the ribs from the spine, and then they ripped out his lungs.'

Ælla of Northumbria (d.867)

Ælla (or Ælle), King of Northumbria, is an extremely obscure figure, given the scarcity of Northumbrian historical sources for this period, although he features in the *Anglo-Saxon Chronicle* and Scandinavian sagas. According to the Saxo Grammaticus (c.1160–c.1220) he captured the Viking Ragnarr Loðbrok and killed him by throwing him into a snake pit. The story goes that Ragnarr's sons – and leaders of the Viking army – Hálfdan and Ívarr (Ivar the Boneless) captured Ælla, torturing him to death with a blood eagle sacrifice. Less colourfully, the *Anglo-Saxon Chronicle* records his death in battle, at York, on 21 March 867.

Historians now largely agree that this type of sacrifice is unlikely to have ever happened, and that the misunderstanding lies in the nature of skaldic verse, a form of poetry which was intended to be both cryptic and associative. The image of the eagle was closely linked with death and blood in Norse mythology, and it has been argued that this device was translated literally by later generations of saga writers, who misunderstood the images of carnivorous birds scavenging battlefields for carrion.

Indeed, if one digs deeply into the sources, the most reliable and earliest mention of a blood eagle comes from the eleventh-century poet Sigvatr Þórðarson, who wrote a verse entitled *Knútsdrápa* dating from between 1020 and 1038 in which he mentioned the killing of Ælla by Ivar the Boneless. It is very limited in its details:

Ok Ellu bak,
At lét hinn's sat,
Ívarr, ara,
Iorví, skorit.

One possible translation is: 'And Ælla's back,/ at had the one who dwelt, / ívarr, with eagle, / York, cut.' An alternative translation is: 'And Ívarr, the one / who dwelt at York, / had Ella's back / cut with [an] eagle.'

These lines, therefore, might refer to the cutting of an eagle onto the back – or they could mean that his back was lacerated by a real eagle. All of the other details, of bones being cut and lungs pulled out as a form of torture, may well be nothing more than a translator's or historian's colourful mistake.

·15·

LUCK

A playing die c.1400 found in Bergen, Norway

*Viking luck is all about
divine protection…*

Rather like the Sámi people, who anthropologists claim have over 1,000 words for reindeer, the Vikings had numerous words for luck – including *gipta*, *gæfa*, *heill*, *fylgja* and *hamingja* – and others that were closely associated with the concept – such as *audna*, *sæla* and *hugr*. Their understanding of luck was correspondingly nuanced, necessarily complicated and indisputably significant.

TYPES OF LUCK

The sagas glitter with references to Viking luck. It might be visible in your appearance as well as in your actions; you could be born with it or you could inherit it; if you were blessed with luck you could even send it to assist someone else. If you were less fortunate, it could be reduced in its potency or you could lose your luck entirely. You could be a generally lucky person or lucky only in specific instances. There was even a rich vocabulary to describe particular kinds of luck. Having the wind in your favour when sailing was referred to as *byrsæll*; for farmers, having the luck of fertility of crops was described as *ársæll*; while *fesæll* meant the luck of cattle if your herd thrived. For warriors, *sigrsæli* meant luck in battle.

For all of this variety, what is certain above all is that luck was immensely powerful, that it could emanate directly from a person, and that if we were to apply our modern understanding of luck – in terms of simple fortuitousness – to the Norse world, we would fall woefully short in our understanding of it.

THUNDERSTONES

The importance of luck in the day-to-day lives of the Vikings meant that it spilled over into their beliefs about the afterlife. It has been argued that one of the ways Vikings hoped to bring luck to their ancestors' journeys in the afterlife was by placing prehistoric stone tools in their graves. These objects, usually axes, were known to the Vikings as 'thunderstones', and were believed to have been created in the sky by lightning before falling to the earth as a stone.

The reasons for interring thunderstones with the deceased have been much debated. It is possible that they served as a lucky charm to protect against lightning, but it is also believed that they were seen as a direct link to Thor, the god of thunder, who could bestow 'luck' by protecting people against chaos and mischief with his hammer Mjölnir – the crushing power of which was responsible for making the lightning as it flew across the sky. It is possible that this is why many of the thunderstones discovered in graves are hammer- or axe-shaped.

A fascinating account from 1868 brings to life the strength of these beliefs. The early-twentieth-century Danish archaeologist Christian Blinkenberg recorded a number of conversations concerning thunderstones. One records how a man travelling in Denmark:

> came into a house of an old woman... and asked to buy
> a polished flint axe which I knew she had found. But
> it was not possible to get it from her. I explained to
> her that it was a tool from the Stone Age. The woman
> replied that I could not make her believe that. No, it was
> a thunderbolt, and when they had a stone like that in
> the house, the lightning would not strike it... The flint
> axe had been found by her near an old willow, a short
> distance from the house; the willow was split, and the

woman believed that the thunderstone she found there had been the cause.

The reluctance of this nineteenth-century Danish woman to part with her find demonstrates the way in which Viking beliefs continued down the centuries. Such stones would be kept in a particular place that was free from daily disturbance, in particular from being touched – sometimes they were bricked into a wall, or laid under the floor or under the roof.

LUCKY HAMMERS

Thunderstones were not the only hammer-like objects linked to Thor and to luck. Archaeologists have unearthed amulets in the form of Thor's hammer in their hundreds across northern Europe. Numerous explanations have been suggested as to why these hammers were worn, but some historians focus on the direct link to the god of thunder, the aura of power and strength that this fostered and the luck that came with it.

Some of these amulets are rough imitations of a hammer, while others are beautifully crafted and decorated. The majority of the hammers discovered are simple, made of silver or lead. Particularly unusual are those made from amber, a resin that was both difficult to acquire and work with. Despite its rarity, a number of surviving examples have been found, including a striking one discovered in a hearth in Viking Dublin that has been dated to the late ninth century, another from the Viking trading town of Hedeby, and one from the Baltic port of Gdańsk – evidence not only of a shared belief in the power of such an amulet but also in the scale of the Viking trade in amber, sought after since ancient times as a semi-precious gem.

A Thor's Hammer made from amber, excavated from the Viking trading settlement in Hedeby, Denmark, currently exhibited in the Viking Museum Haithabu

Baltic amber

The Baltic contains the world's largest deposit of amber and led to the creation of one of Europe's most important trade routes: the 'Amber Road', which ran from the Baltic to the Mediterranean by way of the Vistula and Dnieper rivers. Baltic amber is not only mined, but also 'fished', as winter storms throw chunks of amber out onto the coast.

One of the most valuable finds for historians is also one of the most recently discovered. In 2014, a metal detectorist hunting on the Danish island of Lolland discovered a tiny hammer-shaped amulet dating from the 900s. Just 2.5 centimetres long and cast in bronze, it has traces of silver and gold plating and is important for its runic inscription – which, uniquely among the thousands of hammer-shaped artefacts, specifically identifies the object as a hammer, shutting down debate as to what it might or might not be. It is now a treasured item in the collections of the National Museum of Denmark.

THE UNLUCKY

Perhaps inevitably, for all of their fascination with luck, the Vikings were also interested in lucklessness, and they attributed a number of different events or circumstances to its creation, such as the slaying of kin, oath-breaking and sacrilege. Those cursed by bad luck, however, were not necessarily ostracized; it was, for example, perfectly possible to be both honourable *and* unlucky.

One pretender to the throne in twelfth-century Norway even gained the nickname 'the unlucky'. This was Olaf Gudbrandsson, who seized the Norwegian throne when the incumbent ruler Earl Erling Skakke – who effectively reigned during the minority of Magnus V – was away in Denmark. When Erling returned, Olaf seemed to have everything in his favour: a greater force, the benefit of surprise from a betrayal, and a battle which went his way as Erling's army suffered many dead and wounded. Luck, however, was not on Olaf's side, and Erling (himself wounded in battle) still managed to escape. It proved to be Olaf's only chance to wrest power; the following year he was forced to flee, and subsequently died in Denmark.

Erling Skakke (1115–79)

A Norwegian noble famed for travelling to the Holy Land on crusade between 1152 and 1155, when he received a sword wound to the neck. The wound forced him to hold his head at an angle for the rest of his life – hence *skakke*, meaning 'slanted'.

This is an important example in the history of Viking luck because of what it tells us about one of the forms that luck took. About the failed coup, a saga author commented: 'And this, men said: that Olaf and his followers had shown but little luck in the fight, so surely as Erling's party were given into their hands, if they had but acted with more wisdom.' Here, 'luck' is the difference between a wise plan well executed and a poorly laid one failing; it takes the form of a divine blessing resulting from sound judgement and prudence.

MAKING YOUR OWN LUCK

Not everyone relied on divine intervention; some made their own luck. A gaming die recently excavated from the Vågsbunnen district of Bergen in Norway – specifically from a medieval wooden street dating back to the 1400s in what was a densely populated area of inns – appeared to archaeologists to be a normal two-centimetre cubed wooden die, until they studied the pips (dots) closely. Rather than the six sides ranging from one to six as you might expect, this die consisted of a three, two fives and two fours, and a six – no one or two.

There are two possible explanations: either it was a die used for an unknown game in which it was necessary to have more fives and fours, or – more tantalizingly – it was made for cheating in a number-counting dice game in which fours and fives were an advantage. Logic suggests the former: why have a dice that is so obviously unfair? The two fours and two fives are *not* on opposite sides, making it clear to anyone sitting around the table that the dice was flawed. Historical evidence, however, suggests the latter: we know that betting was such a big problem in Bergen that the authorities banned it. According to a city law of 1276, the King's Ombudsmen could confiscate money on a gambling table and fine the participants half a mark (about 107 grams of silver). Or perhaps the answer instead is that it was a simple mistake, that it was made by a tired and distracted dice-maker, down on his luck.

·16·
FRIENDSHIP

A drinking scene depicted on a Gotland stone

Viking friendship is all about keeping society together...

ODIN'S ADVICE

We know a surprising amount about Viking friendship and the ways in which it bound together Viking society. One of the key sources is *Hávamál*, an anonymous poem that dates from the thirteenth century and includes all sorts of practical advice and wisdom that was said to have come directly from Odin himself.

Hávamál is chock-full of lyrical clues about the interpersonal bonds that tied Vikings to one another. Here in particular we have a verse that offers interesting advice on supporting a network of friends. The power of the verse lies in its simplicity as it expounds an honour code of friendship:

> To his friend a man should be a friend
> and to his friend's friend too;
> but a friend no man should be
> to the friend of his enemy.

It makes explicitly clear that an apparently simple relationship between two people could have far-reaching consequences. Being a loyal friend was greatly valued, as was extending the bond to friends of friends. In other words, ties of fellowship, loyalty and trust cemented Viking society together. But the verse also carries with it a robust warning to draw the line at befriending your enemy's friends, which was synonymous with disloyalty.

The protocols are dealt with elsewhere in *Hávamál*, including instructions on forging such relationships. This was best achieved by the giving of gifts, an act which would allow you to 'mix your soul' with your potential friend, and which was always to be reciprocated. Gift-giving was important because it made the creation of a Viking friendship a public gesture rather than a private act, and once it began it could not stop, as each new gift renewed and sustained the existing relationship. As the poem relates:

> With weapons and clothes friends should gladden one another,
> that is most obvious;
> mutual givers and receivers are friends for longest,
> if the friendship is going to work at all.

Elsewhere in the poem it is made clear that these gifts need not be lavish: 'half a slice of bread' or a 'half-empty tankard' would suffice. In Viking society it was the thought that counted. Other sections advocate regular personal visits and the sharing of food to forge trust, while another stanza has the oft-seen twist of Viking life – the ruthlessness that was never far from the surface:

> To his friend a man should be a friend
> and repay gifts with gifts;
> laughter a man should give for laughter
> and repay treachery with lies.

The message was straightforward: give in return similar to what you receive. Friendship was returned with friendship; treachery and deceit were repaid with enmity and untruths.

VIKING BEST FRIENDS

This is not simply to reduce friendship to a series of mutually beneficial alliances bereft of the emotional core of true feelings. One of the most touching tales of Viking friendship is that shared between a warrior, Gunnar Hámundarson, and a lawyer, Njál Þorgeirsson, as depicted in *Brennu-Njáls saga*.

Brennu-Njáls saga

The Saga of Burnt-Njál was written c.1270-90 and describes events taking place between 960 and 1020 which survived in oral tradition. It is the longest and most intricately developed of all the surviving sagas, and is particularly useful to historians for its treatment of blood feuds, omens and prophecies.

Gunnar and Njál are fast friends who visit each other alternately each winter, and their story begins with Njál offering Gunnar professional advice regarding a thorny problem Gunnar is trying to solve for one of his female relatives. Then, as Gunnar prepares to travel abroad, he asks Njál to help his mother on her farm in his absence. Njál agrees and Gunnar thanks him with gifts. Their friendship is then sorely tested when Gunnar marries a mischief-making, deceitful and murderous woman named Hallgerður. She reveals her intentions in a quote worthy of Shakespeare. When Gunnar orders her not to be aggressive to his friends, she replies 'the trolls take your friends'.

From this moment on, Hallgerður starts to destroy the friends' relationship slowly, beginning with merely insulting Njál, but then she incites one of her servants, named Kolur, to kill one of Njál's servants. This act leads to a whirlwind of retribution and feuding, the exact opposite of good friendship. The following year, a servant of Njál's wife kills Kolur in retaliation. And the murders continue tit for tat, with deaths in each household.

All the while, however, Njál and Gunnar maintain their steadfast friendship, despite the challenges that Hallgerður puts in their way. They always judge the murders fairly and compensate each other financially for the crimes committed, in line with how Viking society sought to regulate unsanctioned violence by economic means – with the payment of a *wergild* (literally 'man price') if someone was injured or killed, or property was stolen. Thus carefully handled, the relationship between the two men continues through economic strife until the death of Gunnar, which occurs because, for once, he chooses not to follow the advice of his friend.

FEASTING AND FRIENDSHIP

There were numerous official occasions for renewing and strengthening friendships, most notably at seasonal feasts. For those of high status these took place in enormous halls, up to fifty metres long and fourteen metres wide. The feasts included *Jól*, a twelve-day feast for the Norse New Year, beginning at the winter solstice in December; *Ostara*, a festival of the spring goddess at the March equinox; the Midsummer festival at the summer solstice; and *Lithasblot*, the harvest festival at the start of August. These feast days were so important to Viking life that they survived the Scandinavian conversion to Christianity, albeit under different names.

Births, funeral feasts and weddings were also important social occasions in which communities gathered together to remember their past and safeguard their future. Such feasting was also a demonstration of power, measured by the number of people present. In both Norway and Iceland, powerful leaders were described as *vinsælir*, literally meaning 'a person rich in friends'.

A significant part of such feasting was the ceremonial consumption of alcohol, which helped engender friendship and alliances by giving extra weight to the words that were exchanged. The drinks were primarily mead (made from honey), beer (made from barley, sometimes with hops) and a type of fruit wine. Real wine, made from grapes, was also consumed, but this was imported from abroad.

THE ARCHAEOLOGY OF FRIENDSHIP

Fascinating archaeological evidence of this ritualized drinking survives, in the form of various vessels and paraphernalia associated with alcohol. These include wine strainers, glass beakers and ladles – as well as drinking horns made from both cattle and goat horn, which were sometimes even decorated with fittings made from precious metals.

No surviving example of drinking paraphernalia from the Viking Age is more impressive than the silver-gilt drinking horn fittings discovered in the Sutton Hoo ship burial, though the find slightly pre-dates the Viking Age. These intricately made decorations would have been mounted on auroch's horns, and show off interlacing animal designs to extraordinary effect – with a bird's head for the tip of the horn.

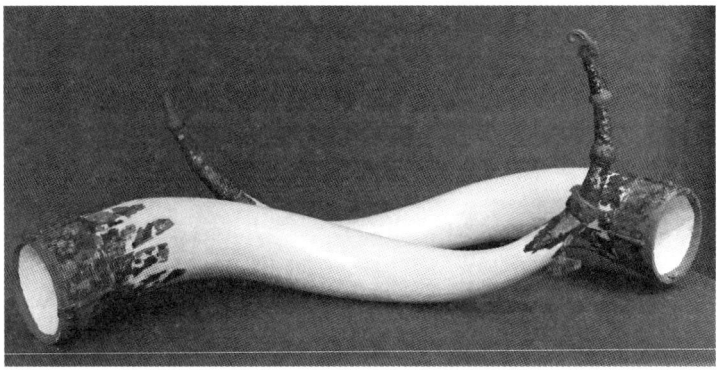

The silver-gilt drinking horn fittings found at the Sutton Hoo ship burial, fitted onto replica horns

Archaeology also provides a powerful sense of how these may have been used in practice. The most compelling evidence is the stone carvings from Gotland, a number of which are known as 'welcoming scenes' and depict a woman, bearing a drinking

Sutton Hoo ship burial

One of the most important archaeological discoveries ever made, and now on display in the British Museum. A mound on the banks of the River Deben in Suffolk dating from c.630, it contained the grave of an Anglo-Saxon king – probably Rædwald (c.599–c.624), King of the East Angles. The oak ship itself did not survive in the acidic soil, but could be clearly seen in the pattern of nails and marks left by the timber in the sand. The grave goods are spectacular, and are now one of the centrepieces of the British Museum's displays.

horn, greeting a man or a group of men, who drink communally with horns apparently raised in a toast. These are potent scenes that sing to us down the centuries of the splendours of Viking camaraderie. And of course a horn, once filled, cannot be set down, which leads us to believe that much of this fellowship was played out with cup in hand.

·17·

FUN

The Lewis chessmen, c.1150–1200

Viking fun is all about strategy…

THE ARCHAEOLOGY OF FUN

Some of the best evidence we have of Viking fun comes from the material record: dice, gaming pieces and gaming boards are all numerous and important archaeological finds. The boards have survived either as independent objects – often double-sided with boards for different games on either side – or carved on the tops of wooden chests. And a number of early medieval shipwrecks have demonstrated that these games were played at sea as well as on land.

The Vikings played a wide range of games, including *tablut*, which we might recognize today as a form of backgammon; *hnefatafl*, a game of strategy that predates chess; and nine men's morris, another game of strategy with ancient roots. These kinds of games linked fun and function. While on the one hand they were pastimes to while away the hours, on the other they had a more serious purpose: to teach and develop strategy. Here again, the archaeological evidence is particularly telling. Among the goods buried with a warrior in a grave uncovered at Birka in Sweden was a very full collection of weaponry alongside gaming pieces. For the Vikings, fun and fighting – and games and strategy – went hand in hand.

GAMING PIECES

Gaming pieces offer historians a wealth of information about Viking art, culture and society, as well as manufacturing techniques, international trade and access to natural resources. They were made from a wide variety of materials: glass, amber, bone, bronze, wood, antler, soapstone, teeth, horn, whalebone, walrus tusk and jet. Working with each type of material required mastery of a different technique, testifying to the wide-ranging skills of Viking craftsmen. The pieces themselves range from small, smooth, undercoated pieces to the most extraordinary pieces of them all – the Lewis chessmen.

Discovered in 1831 – as part of a hoard buried in a small stone chamber in a bank of sand in the Outer Hebrides, Scotland – they still rank as one of the most important examples of early medieval art ever discovered. They represent an extraordinary meeting of cultures: the game of chess originated in India around 600 CE, and came via the Islamic world to Europe, where it was adopted and then adapted to reflect contemporary society. These pieces represent a uniquely Viking take on the game.

Seventy-eight chessmen were found in the Lewis hoard, believed to represent at least four separate sets. This, along with their pristine condition, suggests they may have been the stock of a trader. It is thought that they were crafted in Nidaros (Trondheim) in Norway, around 1150–1200, and it has been suggested that the chess trader was travelling from Norway to Viking Ireland via Scotland, which was then Norwegian territory. The reason that the chessmen were buried remains unknown.

The pieces are exquisitely carved from walrus ivory and whales' teeth into the form of kings, queens, knights and warders (rooks), all with a cartoon-like appearance. A rook in the form of a Berserker bites his shield and brandishes his sword with crazy eyes; a queen sits hunched and pensive, her face resting in her palm; a knight, mounted and armed, peers forward at the oncoming threat. These caricatures represent stock figures within Norse society.

THE STATUS OF FUN

The intricacy of the Lewis pieces suggests that the skill of their creation would have been admired, and that the ownership of such art was a status symbol. We know that skill in playing games of all types was revered. In the saga *Morkinskinna* it is related that, in the year 1113, the dual kings of Norway – King Eysteinn and King Sigurðr – compared their accomplishments. Sigurðr drew attention to his ability at swimming and his strength, but Eysteinn noted: 'That is true, but I am more skilled and better at board games, and that is worth as much as your strength.'

It is notable that the majority of gaming pieces have been discovered in high-status grave excavations, and no fewer than thirty-six ship burials include game boards in the grave goods. For the elite, these games would have been a way of passing the time, but they were also a platform for social bonding and diplomacy at the top levels of society. By interring these games with the deceased, the status of a good strategic game-player in life was commemorated, and their skill was also made available in the afterlife.

Morkinskinna

An Icelandic saga written c.1200 which covers the rule of the Kings of Norway from approximately 1030 until 1177. It is particularly valuable to historians for its colourful descriptions of poets and adventurers who visited the royal courts of Scandinavia. It is also an unusually fine source of Viking proverbs. Its name means 'rotten parchment', for its unusual singed, black and rotten condition. It is now kept at the Royal Library in Copenhagen.

THE VIKING BALL GAME

The Vikings also spent a great deal of time playing physical games that mimicked combat. These included wrestling matches, pillow fighting and even 'drowning matches', in which the fight took place in waist-deep water and the aim was to hold the opponent down until they surrendered. These intensely boisterous games were of course played for fun, but they were also about the strategies of combat.

One such game was a ball game that was a clear mix of fun and fighting, and was called, creatively, *knattleikr* ('ball-game'). We know quite a lot about it because it was described in the sagas, though its intricacies remain tantalizingly beyond our grasp – our understanding of it is based on a bewildering mixture of observations.

We know, for example, that *knattleikr* was violent; that the ball travelled hard and fast and could cause injury. In *Grettis saga,* for example, it is quoted that Grettir, running with the ball towards Audun, 'put the ball right forward in his forehead, so that it broke the skin'. The game could be played on ice, but ice was not necessary for it to be played.

Grettis saga

A complex Icelandic saga written c.1320, it explores the character of a hero with a phenomenal temper: Grettir Ásmundarson, an Icelandic outlaw. The saga is particularly valuable for its descriptions of Viking curses, magic, witchcraft, monsters and ghosts.

We also know that the game was enjoyed by spectators; that it was played with sticks that were used to both hit and catch the ball (though it is unclear how many balls were in play at once – or, indeed, if everyone had a stick); and that the ball could be 'in' or 'out' of bounds. It is likely that the ball was relatively hard and small in order to travel far and fast, perhaps the size of a cricket ball or baseball.

What we do not know is what the balls were made of – though stuffed balls made of several pieces of leather have been found in excavations in Viking York. Nor do we know how many players were required or if the players were somehow organized in positions or pairs; there was certainly a strong one-on-one competitive component. One overriding impression from the historical sources is that there do not appear to have been many hard and fast rules: it seems to have been part game, part chase, part fight.

The finest description comes from *Sigrgarðs saga frækna*:

Melsnati hit the ball over Hogni's head, [so that] he was long in pursuing it. Hogni went after the ball and carried [it back] quickly, then Ulfr caught the ball and threw it at Sigmundr. It hit [him] on the upper jaw bone and the skin was broken. And that was a bad wound. Sigmundr threw the ball at Melsnati, but Ulfr jumped in front and grabbed the ball and threw it at Hogni. Hogni caught the ball, Melsnati jumped on Sigmundr, [and the game became a fist-fight].

Such a transition from playing to fighting, often to single combat, was common. In one description of *knattleikr*, the Berserker and blacksmith Skalla-Grímr became so enraged that he killed one of his opponents and also a female observer.

FEMALE FUN

For all of this surprising knowledge of how the Vikings amused themselves, there are still many gaps, and we know much less about what women did for fun. Viking women were present at some male sports – like the ball game – but only as spectators, and they were entirely absent from others such as horse fights, which were deemed too dangerous. Ordinary women did not play chess.

Horse fights

Known as *hestavíg*, horse fighting was an important form of entertainment held during the summer and autumn months. It is believed to have originated in Norway, though no descriptions of what it actually entailed survive. We know about it from indirect mentions in the sagas, and laws passed concerning its conduct.

Women did have the opportunity to take part in the customary pastime of *tvimenningr* (or 'drinking in pairs'), in which two people sitting apart from the rest of the company drank together from the same cup – an indicator of special comradeship, friendship or love. Ordinarily, however, women drank from their own horns rather than the communal ones passed around the male Vikings, and they were not part of boastful male drinking competitions. Their only role in Viking drinking games was as servers.

Women are often marginalized in historical records, which tend to privilege male experience, but we can sketch women's leisure pursuits through close reading of the sources and paying attention to the gaps and silences. When allowed time outside the daily grind of survival, women were involved in embroidery, storytelling and composing poetry, which we know could be very strategic as ways of exerting power within the household. They also swam – not just for exercise but as a sport – and in the sagas, men and women are occasionally seen playing board games together.

·18·
DOUBLE STANDARDS

Silver figure of Viking woman, found at Tissø, Denmark

Viking double standards are all about sex…

SEX

Throughout much of history, the crucial test of patriarchy – the system by which men assume power and subordinate women – was a society's attitudes surrounding marriage and sexual behaviour. In many places in the past, female chastity and fidelity were fiercely policed, while male sexual prowess outside of the marital bed was by contrast tolerated – and even celebrated in certain circles.

In the Viking Age there was certainly a sexual double standard, with one rule for men and another for women. Women's sexuality was rigidly controlled, and those who committed marital infidelity were severely punished. Things were completely different for pagan Viking husbands, who were able to bring mistresses into the household. Historians point out the prevalence of concubines and extramarital affairs in the literary sources, especially the sagas that focus on family life and family history.

This prevalence of extramarital sexual relations within pagan Viking society explains the introduction of Christian laws in thirteenth-century Scandinavia which sought to define marital fidelity by ruling that the correct place for sex in the eyes of the Church was between a husband and wife. In 1275, the Icelandic bishop Árni's prurient *New Christian Law* for Norway and Iceland distinguished between fornication (sex outside of marriage), which it described as 'single whoredom', and adultery (sex between a married person and someone other than their spouse), which it deemed to be worse and described as 'double whoredom'. The work also distinguished between a man taking a woman as his wife or for his 'bodily lust'.

The Church, of course, was deeply critical of such behaviour. In a series of letters in the late twelfth century, the Norwegian archbishop Eysteinn Erlendsson rebuked Icelandic leaders 'who have left their wives and taken mistresses instead. Some keep both their wives and mistress under their roof and live such unholy lives that it tempts all Christian men to sin.' Another letter blasted male rulers for their treatment of women: 'You, the most famous of men, disgracefully lead lives of cattle, paying no heed to matrimony, although you know that it is a holy bond that must not be broken.'

Eysteinn Erlendsson (d.1188)

Archbishop of Nidaros (modern Trondheim, Norway) from 1161 to his death. Of noble birth, his grandfather was adviser to several Norwegian kings. After his appointment by Pope Alexander III, Eysteinn travelled to Rome and thereafter strengthened the link between the Church of Norway and Rome. Eysteinn is best known for writing a history of Olav II, King of Norway from 1015 to 1028, whose sainthood in 1164 played a major part in the Christianization of Scandinavia.

But while Christian leaders sought to regulate the sexual behaviour of men, especially chieftains, they reserved the harshest treatments for women who had – in their minds – sexually transgressed. Married women found guilty of adultery were charged hefty fines, while husbands remained exempt. The *New Christian Law* stipulated that a wife was to be fined three marks for fornication, while secular law stated that 'if a wife sleeps with a man while married to her husband' she might lose her entire inheritance – in other words, sleeping with a man other than her husband could lead to her utter undoing.

Other punishments imposed by the Church for extramarital bed-swerving chastised women severely. If an unmarried woman died during childbirth, for example, her funeral procession would be denied the presence of a woman carrying a candle at its head (a traditional practice at the funerals of married women). The Church was less harsh in its sanctions against men. Dying men who lived with concubines were refused the Eucharist unless they married or left the woman, but unmarried women in similar circumstances were denied the last rites. The misogyny of churchmen thus refused women eternal salvation, condemning them to an eternity in hell.

THE BALANCE OF POWER

Viking women were also subordinate to men in terms of power. Women's consent, for example, was not required for marriage. If a woman's suitor and her family came to an arrangement and decided upon a match, the woman was powerless to oppose their wishes.

Saga literature does offer examples of daughters who expressed an opinion on marriages, however. In *Laxdæla saga*, Þorgerðr answers her father:

> I have often heard you say that you love me best of all your children, but now it seems to me you make that a falsehood if you wish me to marry the son of a bonds-woman, however goodly and great a dandy he may be.

But while there are examples of girls who challenged paternal authority, in almost all cases the daughters married anyway. And, once wed, women could not appear in court, which further circumscribed their power. This is not, however, to suggest that

Viking women were powerless, and scholars have been quick to point out the different opportunities available for women to exert authority and influence. The realities of everyday life allowed them to carve out areas of responsibility.

Marriage itself allowed women to accrue authority, and their social standing and reputation reflected their husband's place within the world. Women also brought property and goods with them into the marriage. Even those whose husbands had concubines in the marital home had ultimate responsibility for the household, as well as authority over these new women.

Denied political office, the main location of female activity and the centre of their social and economic authority was therefore the household, and raiding and seafaring – from which women were largely excluded – created the circumstances in which that authority might flourish. With the men away from home for long periods of time, women were left in charge of farming and trading, both of which were family-based businesses. Household duties would have involved bringing in the harvest – ensuring the very survival of the family – as well as general housework and cooking, spinning and weaving, childbearing and breastfeeding, and caring for young and old.

It is clear that women were valued for the contribution they made in the domestic sphere. In a runic inscription on a commemorative stone from Hassmyra, Sweden, a husband praises his deceased wife Odindisa for her role as mistress of their farm. It reads 'The good yeoman Holmhöt had this stone raise to Odindisa his wife', accompanied by a verse:

> There will not come to Hassmyra a better mistress who holds sway over the farm. Balle the Red cut these runes. To Sigmund was Odindisa a good sister.

Perhaps surprisingly, divorce was reasonably easy to obtain for women who were unhappy in marriage, as is clear not only from the Icelandic sagas but also early Christian laws. When the

Arab emissary Ibrahim ibn Yaqub al-Tartushi visited Hedeby in Jutland, he was surprised by 'the right of the women to divorce their husbands whenever they like'.

There were also opportunities to exercise power in indirect and informal ways. Take, for example, the marriage between Gunnar and his wife Hallgerður that features in *Brennu-Njáls saga*. In one of the chapters, Gunnar slaps his wife for stealing from a neighbouring farm during a famine, a violent act that Hallgerður remembers for a long time and vows to pay him back for one day. Years later, when Gunnar is attacked by an armed band at home, he holds them off with arrows until an attacker cuts the strings of his bow. Calling to his wife to give him two locks of her hair to replace the severed string, she refuses, reminding him of the slap he once gave her. Her refusal leads to the overpowering and death of her husband.

FEMALE WARRIORS?

In terms of warriors, the Vikings may not have exercised double standards to the same extent as they did in the home. There are examples of female warriors in the sagas, in the guise of valkyries and shield-maidens who fought alongside men in battle, though historians disagree over whether they existed in reality. What we can say with confidence is that women occasionally wielded weapons in attacks on the home.

More recently, however, archaeologists have been arguing for real-life female Viking warriors. The case rests on DNA analysis conducted on a skeleton in a well-furnished grave in the Viking Age town of Birka. Swedish researchers claim that the skeleton is in fact female, rather than male as previously thought. What is unusual about the grave is that the woman's body was buried with an assortment of weapons, including a sword, an axe, a spear, armour-piercing arrows, a battle knife, two shields and two horses – the equipment of a professional warrior. Moreover, the presence of gaming pieces suggests a knowledge of tactics and strategy, which has led researchers to the conclusion that this person was also a high-ranking officer.

The evidence at first sight seems persuasive, but others have expressed a degree of scepticism, asking the question: would it have been possible for a woman to be buried with weaponry and not be a warrior?

While this is not to say unequivocally that there were no female warriors in the past, it is just to add a note of caution, and a recognition that, though we are uncertain whether female warriors existed in the Viking Age, we *are* certain that double standards predominated throughout Viking society.

·19·
SILK

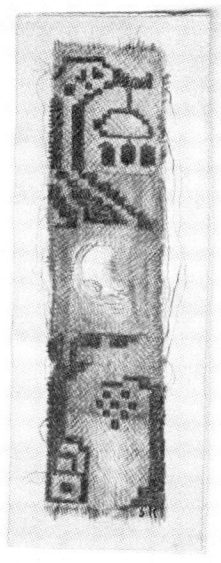

Fragment of silk from the Oseberg ship burial showing the
Shahrokh ('King') bird with a pearl tiara in its beak

*Viking silk is all about the politics
of central Asia...*

A surprising amount of Viking silk survives, having been discovered in good condition and in abundance in numerous ship burials. The Vikings tended to cut it into strips to decorate the edges of clothing. In one burial alone, at Oseberg, fifteen different silk textiles were found and there were more than 100 fragments in total, some with thin strips of hammered gold wrapped around the threads.

This means that we know a great deal about Viking silk – its quality, how it was made and where it came from – which in turn opens up a remarkable window onto the Viking world, especially trade routes and political relations with central Asia.

ACQUIRING SILK

It is believed that the Vikings made their own silk textiles using imported thread, but the majority of silk so far discovered in Scandinavia was originally made outside the region. There are a number of ways it could have come to be there.

It might have been purchased in Persia or the Byzantine empire as part of the far-reaching and well-established trading network between the Viking world and the East, or it could have been given as a high-ranking gift. Olga, the ruler of the Kievan Rus from 945 to 960, travelled to Constantinople in 948–9 to be baptized and negotiate marriage with the Emperor Constantine VII. Before she left – as reported in *The Russian Primary Chronicle*, a contemporary account – he gave her many gifts of gold, silver, silks and vases, in return for which he was expecting 'slaves, wax, and furs, and dispatch soldiery to aid me'. Silk therefore clearly played an important part in gift-giving rituals at a diplomatic level.

Constantine VII (905–59)

One of the most intelligent and well educated of Byzantine emperors, and among the most useful for historians. He wrote four books, including a manual on domestic and foreign policy for his son, Romanos II; a book on ceremonial protocol at the Byzantine court; a book on recent events in the imperial provinces; and a biography of his grandfather, Basil I (811–86).

Silk also played an important role in the Christian Church at this time, as it was used for wall hangings, curtains, altar cloths, manuscript bindings, cushions, and most notably the wrapping of sacred relics. The finest collection of Christian silks from this period comes from the Frankish Benedictine monastery in Chelles near Paris, founded by Queen Bathilde in 658–9 and occupied continuously until it was abandoned during the French Revolution, in 1792. The collection, now in the Musée Alfred-Bonno in Chelles, is particularly important because it offers a glimpse of the beauty and variety of silks that Viking raiders may have discovered – and taken back to Scandinavia – in their raids on European Christian buildings.

POLITICAL CONTROL

Interestingly, Viking silk so far discovered is not of the very best quality. This is a powerful indicator of the strict controls that were placed on the manufacture and sale of silk throughout Persia, with the finest fabric being reserved for royalty and the highest-ranking civil servants. The sale of silk was also controlled in Byzantium, but in a different way. There it was the quantity, rather than the quality, that was restricted. No foreign trader was allowed to buy more than ten *numismata*'s worth of silk – slightly less than the price of a horse.

Regardless of its quality, however, in Viking lands silk was considered a high-status material, and thus it has only been discovered in graves alongside high-value grave goods. In Scandinavia, silk was restricted to the exclusive groups that had the means to acquire it – in terms of both money and connections with the wider world.

A DANGEROUS JOURNEY

By the time silk arrived in Scandinavia, it had travelled thousands of miles from its original production area. Viking traders travelled east and south, towards the Baltic and Black seas via the Volkhov, Lovat, Dnieper, Volga and Don river systems. From there, they made their way to Constantinople and then further south to the Arab world – or east to the commercial hub of Bolghar, capital of the historic Bulgar state and one of the most significant trading cities of the time. The distance that the silk would have travelled invested the material with a powerful exoticism that could have been considered beneficial.

The production centres of Baghdad and Constantinople were constant political, cultural and religious rivals. And the lands through which the silk had to pass were frequently in conflict. The politics of central Asia in the eighth to tenth centuries was unpredictable, violent and bewilderingly complex. In the eighth century, the silk trade was thrown into turmoil by the Arab conquest of central Asia, and almost everywhere a patchwork of kingdoms, empires and nomadic tribes fought each other and amongst themselves. This meant that the likelihood of silk actually reaching Scandinavia was reduced, and that it was a material which was unmistakably associated with – and perhaps even empowered by – the scent of danger.

A MIX OF STYLES

Baghdad and Constantinople may have been game-pieces in the imperial rivalry between the Abbasid Caliphate and Byzantine empire, but the silk-makers still exchanged patterns and technology – and that mixture of styles and manufacturing techniques is visible in the silks discovered in Viking graves.

Perhaps most interesting of all is the way that the patterns reveal layers of time. Before the rise and spread of the Abbasids, the area around Iran was ruled by the Sassanid dynasty (224–651), the last kingdom of the Persian empire. The Sassanids had a highly distinctive and influential silk-making tradition. Even after their defeat to the Abbasids and subsequent fall, silk production in Sassanian factories continued, and the 'old' designs continued to be made and sold abroad – even under the new Abbasid rulers. Some of these designs made it to Scandinavia.

Abbasid Caliphate

The Abbasids were not direct descendants of the Prophet Muhammad, being descended from his uncle al-'Abbas (c.619–c.653). From 718, this aggressive and ambitious family worked to gain control of the empire from the Umayyads, finally ending in open revolt and a battle in 750 when Marwan II, the last Umayyad caliph, was defeated. The capital was moved from Harran to Baghdad, and the empire's focus turned east. The Abbasids were famed for promoting commerce, industry, the arts and science.

Perhaps the finest example is a depiction of a curious bird on silk discovered in the Oseberg ship burial. No normal animal, this is the *Shahrokh* (literally 'kingbird') – a messenger bird from Persian mythology that represented a royal blessing from heaven. The *Shahrokh* has a special place in Persian art: it appears in metalwork and on wall decorations, as well as in silk. It also appears in central Asian art in the area which is now Uzbekistan and Tajikistan – once the kingdom of the Sogdians, who had their origin in the sixth century BCE.

If this piece of silk was produced in the first quarter of the ninth century in or around Baghdad or central Asia, the pattern chosen was not a contemporary one, but an image plucked from history. In this way, Viking silk not only can take us thousands of miles from Scandinavia, but also hundreds of years from the Viking Age, to a different time and place altogether.

·20·

STAFFS

Iron divination staffs belonging to two seeresses

Viking staffs are all about sorcery…

There is a rich literary tradition in Icelandic sagas of women and sorcery. The ability of seeresses to predict the future, cast spells and use supernatural magic was a potent source of female power available to women of the Viking period. What's more, modern archaeologists are now catching up and reinterpreting the material evidence that survives from the period in imaginative ways. A central debate focuses on how we interpret staffs: Were they instruments for stirring or pointing? Or were they in fact... magic wands?

THE FYRKAT WITCH

One of the most remarkable archaeological sites that sheds light on Viking sorcery is the grave of a woman buried in the Danish ring fort of Fyrkat, dating from around 980. The grave has been interpreted as the burial site of a witch or sorceress – a *völva* – because of the unusual range of grave goods that were discovered in the tomb.

She was buried wearing two silver toe rings, which are unique for female burials during this period, and a number of poisonous henbane seeds were also found in the grave. If thrown into a fire, these produce a hallucinogenic smoke – it is possible that such seeds were given to Viking warriors before battle in order to induce the trance-like Berserker state.

Fyrkat ring fortress

Fyrkat is a Viking ring fortress near Hobro in Denmark, dating from c.980, built during the reign of Harald Bluetooth. The fort contained sixteen identical longhouses arranged in four identical squares, several of which have been reconstructed and can be visited. Only seven such ring fortresses have been discovered, and only in Denmark and Sweden. Another example is Trelleborg (see p. 59).

Other objects included a box containing owl pellets and the bones of birds and animals including the lower jaw of a pig; a small silver amulet shaped like a chair – possibly representing the *seid*, the magic chair in which a seeress sat during seances; and a hollow box-brooch that may have been to store 'white lead' – perhaps to be used as a type of face paint – which in concentrated form is poisonous. These were all the accoutrements of someone who practised the supernatural arts and took part in rituals.

Most interesting of all is an iron staff, which was formerly thought to be a cooking spit but has recently been reinterpreted by historians as a divination staff or wand. Sorcery in the Icelandic sagas features the *völva*, whose powers could be used for good or for evil: for seeking out secrets, healing the sick or bringing good luck; or to curse, induce illness, misinform or cause accidents, injury and death.

One of the most vivid descriptions is found in *Eiríks saga rauða*, which recounts a meeting with a woman named Thorbjörg, who we are informed is a prophetess or 'spae-queen'. During winter time, people invited her into their homes either because they were curious about the season or desired to know their fate. When entering any house, she was offered a 'hearty welcome' and a high seat was prepared with a cushion upon which to perch. Moreover, the physical description of the old woman is intriguing, especially in the detailing of the staff which she carried. She was, we are told:

> dressed in such wise that she had a blue mantle over her, with strings for the neck, and it was inlaid with gems quite down to the skirt. On her neck she had glass beads. On her head she had a black hood of lambskin, lined with ermine. A staff she had in her hand, with a knob thereon; it was ornamented with brass, and inlaid with gems round about the knob.

After a night's sleep and being asked to inspect the herd, household and homestead, the next morning the woman would give her predictions for the future.

THE PRINCESS AND THE HIGH PRIESTESS

The Oseberg ship burial has also been linked to sorcery by archaeologists. It contains the burial chamber of two women, one in her mid-twenties and one around fifty years old. In the past, archaeologists identified these two figures as a princess and her slave, but more recent studies have suggested that what we have here is in fact a princess and her high priestess.

The evidence for this intriguing interpretation comes from the grave goods. They include two iron lamps, a purse containing cannabis seeds, a number of carefully carved wooden animal heads and a cart carved with images of cats, which are associated with the Norse goddess Freyja, who was a *seiðr* and travelled in a chariot pulled by two cats. (The image of Freyja recurs in the archaeological evidence of sorceresses' graves.) Most importantly, however, the grave goods include a staff, which has been viewed as a sorceress's wand. Context here is crucial, and the interpretation of these staffs as wands rather than as roasting spits or measuring rods is in large part because of the other grave goods – including narcotics and unusual ritual objects – buried with the deceased.

The staffs or wands found in the graves at Fyrkat and Oseberg are not isolated examples. More than forty similar staffs have been discovered over the last hundred years or so in Viking Age graves throughout Scandinavia and also in Ireland, Iceland and Russia. What makes the identification of these objects as wands even more plausible is that most were found in the graves of high-status women, for whom such wands are known to have been important objects.

Of the iron or bronze staffs that we know about, each is unique but there are some common themes, including bronze mounts or cages on the end of them that are sometimes hung with rings or pendants. A number have small holes drilled in the end which might have taken ribbon or wire, or other organic matter now decayed. Historians have argued that these objects would have been terrifically impressive, with the gleaming bronze mounts offset by black iron shafts – all adding to the charismatic power of the seeresses who owned and perhaps brandished them.

ODIN AND THE SEERESS

Literary echoes of the activities of female sorceresses connected to these iron staffs can be found in the Icelandic sagas. The poem *Völuspá* ('The wise woman's prophecy') narrates the creation of the world and its end through the device of a *völva* speaking to Odin, and refers to a 'prophetic wand'.

In the poem, Odin – disguised as a poor old man – visits a seeress wishing to know the future and the fate of the world. Recognizing him almost instantly as the great god, the *völva* receives payment of a ring and necklace before relaying to him the story of the creation of the world, the beginning years, the origin of the dwarves, the first man and woman and the first war between the gods. The seeress then tells Odin of the end of the world – a war between the gods and their enemies such as the giants. She tells him of the valkyries, who bring dead warriors to help the gods on the battlefield, and the death of the god Baldr and even the demise of Odin himself, as 'fire leaps high about heaven itself'. Finally, she foretells that the world will rise again, but warns that evil, too, will return. The last stanza of the poem speaks of the rising of a dragon carrying bodies of men:

> From below the dragon | dark comes forth,
> Nithhogg flying | from Nithafjoll
> The bodies of men | on his wings he bears,
> The serpent bright: | but now must I sink.

She awakens from her trance and 'sinks' back into her grave, her secret knowledge and prophecies having been divulged.

JOIN IN!

We believe passionately that everyone – not just professional historians – can effectively exercise their historical imagination. If you have a great idea for a *Histories of the Unexpected* subject, fill in one of these forms, photograph it and send it to us

on Twitter **@UnexpectedPod**

or by email to **info@historiesoftheunexpected.com** and we might dedicate a podcast episode to you and your historical imagination!

The history of _____ is all about…

_____

The history of _____ is all about…

_____

The history of _____ is all about…

_____

The history of _____ is all about…

_____

The history of _____ is all about…

SELECTED FURTHER READING

GENERAL

Arnold, Martin, *The Vikings: Wolves of War* (Lanham, MD: Rowman & Littlefield, 2007).

Christiansen, Eric, *The Norsemen in the Viking Age* (Oxford: Blackwell, 2002).

Ferguson, Robert, *The Vikings: A History* (New York: Penguin Books, 2009).

Hall, Richard, *The World of the Vikings* (London: Thames & Hudson, 2007).

Haywood, John, *The Penguin Historical Atlas of the Vikings* (New York: Penguin Putnam, 1995).

Hreinsson, Vidar, et al., eds, *The Complete Sagas of Icelanders, Including 49 Tales*, 5 vols (Reykjavík: Leifur Eiriksson Publishing, 1997).

Jesch, Judith, *Women in the Viking Age* (Woodbridge, Suffolk: Boydell Press, 1991).

Jones, Gwyn, *A History of the Vikings* (2nd edition) (Oxford: Oxford University Press, 1984).

Logan, F. Donald, *The Vikings in History* (3rd edition) (London: Routledge, 2005).

Oliver, Neil, *The Vikings* (New York: Pegasus Books, 2013).

Pritsak, Omeljan, *The Origin of Rus'* (Cambridge, MA: Harvard University Press, 1981).

Ramirez, Janina, '8 Viking Myths Busted', *History Extra* (August 2015) https://www.historyextra.com/period/viking/8-viking-myths-busted/ [accessed 03.08.18].

Roesdahl, Else, *The Vikings* (2nd edition), trans. Susan M. Margeson and Kirsten Williams (London: Penguin, 1998).

Sawyer, Peter H., *Kings and Vikings: Scandinavia and Europe AD 700–1100* (London: Methuen, 1982).

———, *The Age of the Vikings* (2nd edition) (New York: Palgrave Macmillan, 1972).

Smyth, Alfred P., *Scandinavian Kings in the British Isles, 850–880* (Oxford: Oxford University Press, 1977).

Wilson, David M., *The Vikings and Their Origins: Scandinavia in the First Millennium* (2nd edition) (New York: Thames & Hudson, 1980).

Websites

BBC History, 'The Vikings', http://www.bbc.co.uk/history/ancient/vikings/ [accessed 03.08.18].

Fotevikens Viking Museum, Höllviken, Sweden, https://www.fotevikensmuseum.se/en/ [accessed 03.08.18].

Jorvik Viking Centre, York, www.jorvikvikingcentre.co.uk.

Moesgaard Museum, https://www.moesgaardmuseum.dk/en/ [accessed 03.08.18].

National Museum of Denmark, 'The Viking Age', https://en.natmus.dk/historical-knowledge/denmark/prehistoric-period-until-1050-ad/the-viking-age/ [accessed 03.08.18].

Viking Ship Museum, Roskilde, Denmark, https://www.vikingeskibsmuseet.dk/en/ [accessed 03.08.18].

1. KEYS

Berg, Heidi Lund, '"Truth" and Reproduction of Knowledge: Critical Thoughts on the Interpretation and Understanding of Iron-Age Keys', in Marianne Hem Eriksen et al., eds, *Viking Worlds: Things, Spaces and Movement* (Oxford: Oxbow Books, 2015), pp. 124–42.

Glauser, Jürg, 'Sagas and Space – Thinking Space in Viking Age and Medieval Scandinavia', *European Journal of Scandinavian Studies*, 47/1 (April 2017), pp. 164–7.

Gustafsson, Ny Björn, 'Some Notes on the Production of Norse Padlocks', *Viking Heritage Magazine*, 2 (2004), pp. 12–13.

Jesch, Judith, *Women in the Viking Age* (Woodbridge, Suffolk: Boydell, 1991).

Lindquist, Malin, 'The Key – A Practical Object and Symbol of Power', *Viking Heritage Magazine*, 4 (2005), pp. 8–9.

Milek, Karen, 'The Roles of Pit Houses and Gendered Spaces on Viking-Age Farmsteads in Iceland', *Medieval Archaeology*, 56/1 (January 2012), pp. 85–130.

National Museum of Denmark, 'Housewives as key carriers?', https://en.natmus.dk/historical-knowledge/denmark/

prehistoric-period-until-1050-ad/the-viking-age/the-people/
women/ [accessed 23.08.18].

Steele, Romana Sue, 'Viking Age Keys and Locks: Symbolism in Life
and Death', http://www.gotland-fieldschool.com/lockspaviken.pdf
[accessed 23.08.18].

Tomtlund, J. E., 'Locks and Keys', in W. Holmqvist, ed., *Excavations at
Helgö V: 1 Workshop part II* (Stockholm: Kungliga Vitterhets Historie
och Antikvitets Akademien, 1978), Ch.1.

2. GRAFFITI

Champion, Matthew, *Medieval Graffiti: The Lost Voices of England's
Churches* (London: Ebury Press, 2015).

Daniell, Christopher, 'Graffiti, Calliglyphs and Markers in the UK',
Archaeologies: Journal of the World Archaeological Congress, 7/2 (2011),
pp. 454–76.

McCormick, Finbar, and Ole Kastholm, 'A Viking Ship Graffito from
Kilclief, County Down, Ireland', *The International Journal of Nautical
Archaeology*, 46/1 (March 2017), pp. 83–91.

Mitchiner, Michael, 'Evidence for Viking-Islamic Trade Provided by
Samanid Silver Coinage', *East and West*, 37/1/4 (December 1987), pp.
139–50.

Thomov, Thomas, 'Four Scandinavian Ship Graffiti from Hagia
Sophia', *Byzantine and Modern Greek Studies*, 38/2 (2014), pp. 168–84.

3. NICKNAMES

Costambeys, Marios, 'Erik Bloodaxe [Eiríkr Blóðöx, Eiríkr
Haraldsson]', *Oxford Dictionary of National Biography* (Oxford:
Oxford University Press, 2004).

Gade, Kari Ellen, 'Penile Puns: Personal Names and Phallic Symbols in
Skaldic Poetry', *Essays in Medieval Studies: Proceedings of the Illinois
Medieval Association*, 6 (1989), pp. 57–67.

Orel, Vladimir, *A Handbook of Germanic Etymology* (Leiden,
Netherlands: Brill, 2003).

Peterson, Lena, 'Developments of Personal Names from Ancient
Nordic to Old Nordic', in Oscar Bandle et al., eds, *The Nordic
Languages: An International Handbook of the History of the North
Germanic Languages* (Berlin: Walter de Gruyter, 2002), pp. 664–71.

Peterson, Paul, 'Old Norse Nicknames' (MA thesis, University of

Iceland, 2012), https://skemman.is/bitstream/1946/12799/1/Old%20 Norse%20Nicknames.pdf [accessed 27.08.18].

Whaley, Diana, 'Nicknames and Narratives in the Sagas', *Arkiv för nordisk filologi*, 108 (1993), pp. 122–46.

Willson, Kendra, 'Icelandic Nicknames' (PhD dissertation, University of California Berkeley, 2007).

4. MISCHIEF

'Abbo of Fleury's Life of St. Edmund, King of East Anglia before 870...', in Henry Sweet's *Anglo-Saxon Primer* (9th edition) (Oxford: Oxford University Press, 1961), pp. 81–7.

Andrén, Anders, 'Behind *Heathendom*: Archaeological Studies of Old Norse Religion', *Scottish Archaeological Journal*, 27/2 (2005), pp. 105–38.

Cavill, Paul, 'Fun and Games: Viking Atrocity in the *Passio sancti Eadmundi*', *Notes and Queries*, 52 (September 2005), pp. 284–6.

Cawley, Frank Stanton, 'The Figure of Loki in Germanic Mythology', *The Harvard Theological Review*, 32/4 (1939), pp. 309–26.

Barndon, Randi, 'Sparks of Life: The Concept of Fire in Iron Working', *Current Swedish Archaeology*, 13 (January 2005), pp. 1–19.

Eldar, Heide, 'Loki, the Vätte, and the Ash Lad: A Study Combining Old Scandinavian and Late Material', *Viking and Medieval Scandinavia*, 7 (2011), pp. 63–106.

Wanner, Kevin J., 'Sewn Lips, Propped Jaws, and a Silent Áss (or Two): Doing Things with Mouths in Norse Myth', *The Journal of English and Germanic Philology,* 111/1 (January 2012), pp. 1–24.

———, 'Cunning Intelligence in Norse Myth: Loki, Óðinn, and the Limits of Sovereignty', *History of Religions*, 48/3 (2009), pp. 211–46.

Whitelock, Dorothy, 'Fact and Fiction in the Legend of St Edmund', *Proceedings of the Suffolk Institute of Archaeology*, 31 (1967–9), pp. 217–33.

5. HAIR GROOMING

Ambrosiani, K., *Viking Age Combs, Comb Making and Comb Makers: In the Light of Finds from Birka and Ribe* (Stockholm Studies in Archaeology, 2) (Stockholm: University of Stockholm, 1981).

Arwill-Nordbladh, Elisabeth, 'Viking Age Hair', *Internet Archaeology*, 42 (2016), http://dx.doi.org/10.11141/ia.42.6.8 [accessed 01.08.18].

Ashby, S. P., 'Technologies of Appearance: Hair Behaviour in Early-Medieval Britain and Europe', *Archaeological Journal*, 171 (2014), pp. 153–84.

———, *A Viking Way of Life: Combs and Communities in Britain and Scandinavia, c. AD 800–1100* (Stroud: Amberley, 2014).

———, 'Making a Good Comb: Mercantile Identity in Ninth to Eleventh-Century England', in L. ten Harkel and D. M. Hadley, eds, *Everyday Life in Viking-Age Towns: Social Approaches to Towns in England and Ireland c. 800–1100* (Oxford: Oxbow Books, 2013), pp. 193–208.

———, 'An Atlas of Medieval Combs from Northern Europe', *Internet Archaeology*, 30 (2011), http://intarch.ac.uk/journal/issue30/ashby_index.html [accessed 02.08.18].

Goosmann, Erik, 'The Long-Haired Kings of the Franks: like so many Samsons?', *Early Medieval Europe,* 20/3 (August 2012), pp. 233–59.

Hallpike, C. R., 'Social Hair', *Man*, New Series, 4/2 (June 1969), pp. 256–64.

Kristoffersen, Siv, 'Half Beast–Half Man: Hybrid Figures in Animal Art', *World Archaeology,* 42/2 (2010), pp. 216–72.

Leach, E. R., 'Magical Hair', *The Journal of the Royal Anthropological Institute of Great Britain and Ireland*, 88/2 (1958), pp. 147–64.

Wallace-Hadrill, J. M., *The Long-Haired Kings and Other Studies in Frankish History* (London: Methuen, 1962).

6. HOT SPRINGS AND SAUNAS

Ashby, S. P., 'Technologies of Appearance: Hair Behaviour in Early-Medieval Britain and Europe', *Archaeological Journal*, 171 (2014), pp. 153–84.

Berman, Nina, 'Imperial Narratives: Islamic Concepts of Inclusion and Exclusion in Ibn Fadlan's Account of His Mission to the Bulgars', in Anne R. Richards and Iraj Omidvar, eds, *Historic Engagements with Occidental Cultures, Religions, Powers* (New York: Palgrave Macmillan, 2014), pp. 89–109.

Hermes, Nizar F., 'The Moor's First Sight: An Arab Poet in a Ninth-Century Viking Court', in Richards and Omidvar, *Historic Engagements with Occidental Cultures, Religions, Powers*, pp. 57–69.

Hollander, Lee M., 'The Structure of *Eyrbyggja Saga*', *The Journal of English and Germanic Philology*, 58/2 (1959), pp. 222–7.

Hraundal, Thorir Jonsson, 'The Rus in Arabic Sources: Cultural Contacts and Identity' (unpublished PhD dissertation, University of Bergen, 2013).

Hreinsson, Vidar, et al., eds, *The Complete Sagas of Icelanders, Including 49 Tales*, 5 vols (Reykjavík: Leifur Eiriksson Publishing, 1997).

Nordskog, Michael, and Aaron W. Hautala, *The Opposite of Cold: The Northwoods Finnish Sauna Tradition* (Minneapolis: University of Minnesota Press, 2010).

Page, Raymond Ian, *Chronicles of the Vikings: Records, Memorials, and Myths* (London: British Museum Press, 1995).

Quaritch, B., *The Saga Library: The Story of the Ere-dwellers, with the Story of the Heath-slayings* (London: B. Quaritch, 1892).

Sveinbjarnardóttir, Guðrún, *Reykholt: Archaeological Investigations at a High Status Farm in Western Iceland* (Reykjavík: National Museum of Iceland, 2012).

Vidal, Teva, 'Houses and Domestic Life in the Viking Age and Medieval Period: Material Perspectives from Sagas and Archaeology' (PhD thesis, University of Nottingham, 2013).

7. BREAK-INS

Bill, Jan, and Aoife Daly, 'The Plundering of the Ship Graves from Oseberg and Gokstad: An Example of Power Politics?', *Antiquity*, 86/333 (2012), pp. 808–24.

Drachmann, A. G., 'On Named Swords, Especially in Icelandic Sagas', *Centaurus*, 13/1 (1969), pp. 29–36.

Klevnäs, Alison Margaret, '"Imbued with the Essence of the Owner": Personhood and Possessions in the Reopening and Reworking of Viking-Age Burials', *European Journal of Archaeology*, 19/3 (2016), pp. 456–76.

Lund, Julie, 'Connectedness with Things: Animated Objects of Viking Age Scandinavia and Early Medieval Europe', *Archaeological Dialogues*, 24/1 (June 2017), pp. 89–108.

———, 'Living Places or Animated Objects? Sámi Sacrificial Places with Metal Objects and Their South Scandinavian Parallels', *Acta Borealia*, 32/1 (2015), pp. 20–39.

———, 'Fragments of a Conversion: Handling Bodies and Objects in Pagan and Christian Scandinavia, AD 800–1100', *World Archaeology*, 45/1 (2013), pp. 46–63.

Pearce, Mark, 'The Spirit of the Sword and Spear', *Cambridge Archaeological Journal*, 23/1 (February 2013), pp. 55–67.

van Haperen, M., 'Rest in Pieces: An Interpretative Model of Early Medieval "Grave Robbery"', *Medieval and Modern Matters*, 1 (2010), pp. 1–36.

8. COLOUR

Andersen, Erik, 'Woollen Material For Sails', in Olaf Olsen et al., eds, *Shipshape: Essays for Ole Crumlin-Pedersen on the Occasion of his 60th Anniversary, February 24th 1995* (Roskilde: The Viking Ship Museum, 1995), pp. 249–70.

Biggam, C. P., *The Semantics of Colour: A Historical Approach* (Cambridge: Cambridge University Press, 2012).

Bregnhøi, Line, and Mads Chr. Christensen, *Sagnlandet Lejre: Vikingetidens farvepalet* (Copenhagen: National Museum of Denmark, 2017).

Callmer, Johan, *Trade Beads and Bead Trade in Scandinavia ca. 800–1000 AD* (Bonn: Rudolf Habelt Verlag, 1977).

Christensen, Mads Chr., 'Painted Wood from the Eleventh Century: Examination of the Hørning Plank', in Jilleen Nadolny, ed., *Medieval Painting in Northern Europe* (London: Archetype Publications, 2006).

Delvaux, Matthew C., 'Colors of the Viking Age: A Cluster Analysis of Glass Beads from Hedeby', *Journal of Glass Studies*, 60 (2018), pp. 1–27.

———, 'Patterns of Scandinavian Bead Use between the Iron Age and Viking Age, ca. 600–1000 CE', *Beads: Journal of the Society of Bead Researchers*, 29 (2017), pp. 3–30.

Mannering, Ulla, *Iconic Costumes: Scandinavian Late Iron Age Costume Iconography* (Oxford: Oxbow Books, 2016).

Reed, Michael F., 'Norwegian Stave Churches and their Pagan Antecedents', *RACAR: revue d'art canadienne / Canadian Art Review*, 24/2 (1997), pp. 3–13.

Sindbæk, Søren Michael, 'Northern Emporium: The Archaeology of Network Urbanism in Viking-age Ribe', http://projects.au.dk/northernemporium/ [accessed 29.08.18].

Wolf, Kirsten, 'NonBasic Color Terms in Old NorseIcelandic', in Jeffrey Turco, ed., *New Norse Studies: Essays on the Literature and Culture of Medieval Scandinavia* (Ithaca, NY: Cornell University Library Press, 2015), pp. 389–433.

———, 'Basic Color Terms in Old NorseIcelandic: A Quantitative Study', *Orð og Tunga*, 15 (June 2013), pp. 141–61.

———, 'Some Comments on Old NorseIcelandic Color Terms', *Arkiv för Nordisk Filologi*, 121 (2006), pp. 173–92.

9. TOYS

Callow, C., 'First Steps Towards an Archaeology of Childhood in Iceland', *Archaeologia Islandica,* 5 (2006), pp. 55–96.

Christensen, A., 'Ship Graffiti and Models', in Patrick F. Wallace, ed., *Miscellanea 1, Medieval Dublin Excavations, 1962–81* (Dublin: Royal Irish Academy, 1988), pp. 13–26.

Crawford, S., 'The Archaeology of Play Things: Theorising a Toy Stage in the "Biography" of Objects', *Childhood in the Past,* 2/1 (2009), pp. 55–70.

Hansen, A., 'Representations of Children in the Icelandic Sagas', in S. Würth et al., eds, *Sagas and Societies. International conference at Borgarnes, Iceland, September 5–9, 2002* (University of Tübingen, 2002).

Hedenstierna-Jonson, C., 'She Came from Another Place: On the Burial of a Young Girl in Birka', in Marianne Hem Eriksen et al., eds, *Viking Worlds: Things, Spaces and Movement* (Oxford: Oxbow Books, 2015), pp. 90–101.

Jakobsson, Ármann, 'Troublesome Children in the Sagas of Icelanders', *Saga-Book of the Viking Society,* 27 (2003), pp. 5–24.

Jesch, Judith, *Women in the Viking Age* (Rochester, NY: Boydell Press, 1991).

Kamp, K. A., 'Where Have All the Children Gone?: The Archaeology of Childhood', *Journal of Archaeological Method and Theory,* 8/1 (2001), pp. 1–34.

Khoroshev, A. S., 'Toys and Miniatures', in M. Brisbane and J. Hather, eds, *Wood Use in Medieval Novgorod* (Oxford: Oxbow Books, 2007), pp. 344–53.

McAlister, Deirdre, 'Childhood in Viking and Hiberno-Scandinavian Dublin, 800–1100', in D. M. Hadley and Letty ten Harkel, eds, *Everyday Life in Viking-Age Towns: Social Approaches to Towns in England and Ireland c. 800–1100* (Oxford: Oxbow Books, 2013), pp. 86–102.

Morgan, Rachel, 'Children in Viking Studies: A Case for Material Culture Studies', *The Post Hole,* 46 (2016), http://www.theposthole.org/sites/theposthole.org/files/downloads/posthole_47_356.pdf [accessed 07.07.18].

Orme, Nicholas, *Medieval Children* (New Haven, CT: Yale University Press, 2001).

———, 'The Culture of Children in Medieval England', *Past and Present,* 148/1 (1995), pp. 48–88.

Price, Neil, 'Dying and the Dead: Viking Age Mortuary Behaviour', in Stefan Brink and Neil Price, eds, *The Viking World* (London: Routledge, 2012), pp. 257–73.

Richards, Julian D., *The Vikings: A Very Short Introduction* (Oxford: Oxford University Press, 2005).

van Beek, Gus W., 'The Buzz: A Simple Toy from Antiquity', *Bulletin of the American Schools of Oriental Research*, 275 (1989), pp. 53–8.

Wilkie, L., 'Not Merely Child's Play: Creating a Historical Archaeology of Children and Childhood', in J. S. Derevenski, ed., *Children and Material Culture* (London: Routledge, 2002), pp. 100–14.

10. TEETH

Arcini, Caroline, 'The Vikings Bare their Filed Teeth', *American Journal of Physical Anthropology*, 128/4 (December 2005), pp. 727–33.

Arwidsson, Greta, and Gosta Berg, *The Mästermyr Find: A Viking Age Tool Chest from Gotland* (Lompoc, California: Norm Larson Books, 2000).

Kennedy, Maev, 'Incisor Raiding: Viking Marauders Had Patterns Filed into their Teeth', *The Guardian* [Online], 4 July 2011, https://www.theguardian.com/science/2011/jul/04/teeth-viking-warriors-dorset-grave [accessed 23.06.18].

Kjellström, Anna, 'Spatial and Temporal Trends in New Cases of Men with Modified Teeth from Sweden (AD 750–1100)...', *European Journal of Archaeology*, 17/1 (2014), pp. 45–59.

Loe, Louise, Angela Boyle, Helen Webb and David Score, *'Given to the Ground': A Viking Age Mass Grave on Ridgeway Hill, Dorset* (Oxford: Oxford Archaeology, 2014).

Martens, Irmelin, 'Recent Investigations of Iron Production in Viking Age Norway', *Norwegian Archaeological Review*, 15/1 (1982), pp. 29–44.

Melchior, Linea, Toomas Kivisild, Niels Lynnerup, Jørgen Dissing, 'Evidence of Authentic DNA from Danish Viking Age Skeletons Untouched by Humans for 1,000 Years', *PLoS One*, 3/5 (2008), pp. 1–8.

Mortágua, A., 'Mutilated Teeth: An Analysis of Eleven Vikings from Slite Square, Gotland' (unpublished MA dissertation, Stockholm University, 2006).

Pacey, Laura, 'Viking Teeth Offer Insight into Cultural Status', *British Dental Journal*, 216 (April 2014), p. 445.

Toplak, Matthias S., 'Prone Burials and Modified Teeth at the Viking Age Cemetery of Kopparsvik: The Changing of Social Identities at the Threshold of the Christian Middle Ages', *Analecta Archaeologica Ressoviensia*, 10 (2015), pp. 77–98.

11. DOORS

Andreeff, Alexander, 'Archaeological Excavations of Picture Stone Sites', in Maria Herlin Karnell, ed., *Gotland's Picture Stones: Bearers of an Enigmatic Legacy* (Gotländskt Arkiv, 2012), pp. 129–212.

Andrén, Anders, 'Doors to Other Worlds: Scandinavian Death Rituals in Gotlandic Perspectives', *Journal of European Archaeology*, 1/1 (1993), pp. 33–56.

Eriksen, Marianne Hem, *Architecture, Society, and Ritual in Viking Age Scandinavia: Doors, Dwellings, and Domestic Space* (Oxford: Oxbow Books, 2019).

——, 'The Powerful Ring: Door Rings, Oath Rings and the Sacral Place', in Marianne Hem Eriksen et al., eds, *Viking Worlds: Things, Spaces and Movement* (Oxford: Oxbow Books, 2014), pp. 73-87.

——, 'Doors to the Dead: The Power of Doorways and Thresholds in Viking Age Scandinavia', *Archaeological Dialogues*, 20/2 (December 2013), pp. 187–214.

Feilberg, H. F., 'The Corpse-Door: A Danish Survival', *Folklore*, 18/4 (1907), pp. 364–75.

Klevnäs, Alison Margaret, '"Imbued with the Essence of the Owner": Personhood and Possessions in the Reopening and Reworking of Viking-Age Burials', *European Journal of Archaeology*, 19/3 (2016), pp. 456–76.

Norris, Herbert, 'Supposed Skin of a Viking from Hadstock Church Door', *East Anglian: or Notes and Queries on Subjects Connected with the Counties of Suffolk, Cambridge, Essex and Norfolk*, 11 (January 1906), p. 96.

Unwin, Simon, *Doorway* (London: Routledge, 2007).

12. GOADING

Clover, Carol, 'Hildigunnr's Lament', in John Lindow, Lars Lönnroth and Gerd Wolfgang Weber, eds, *Structure and Meaning in Old Norse Literature: New Approaches to Textual Analysis and Literary Criticism* (Odense, Denmark: Odense University Press, 1985), pp. 141–86.

Hurstwic, 'Honor, Dueling, and Drengskapr in the Viking Age', http://www.hurstwic.org/history/articles/society/text/drengur.htm [accessed 14.09.18].

Jochens, Jenny, *Women in Old Norse Society* (Ithaca, NY: Cornell University Press, 1995).

Laxdaela Saga, trans. Magnus Magnusson and Hermann Falsson (London: Penguin Books, 1969).

Pulsiano, Phillip, '"Danish Men's Words Are Worse than Murder": Viking Guile and "The Battle of Maldon"', *The Journal of English and Germanic Philology*, 96/1 (January 1997), pp. 13–25.

The Saga of Grettir the Strong, trans. Bernard Scudder (London: Penguin Books, 2005).

'The Saga of the People of Kjalarnes', in *The Complete Sagas of the Icelanders*, vol. 3, trans. Robert Cook and John Porter (Reykjavík: Leifur Eiriksson Publishing, 1997).

The Saga of the Volsungs, trans. Jesse Byock (London: Penguin Books, 1999).

Ward, Elizabeth I., 'Completing *Thordur saga hredu*: A Regional Saga in Disguise', *Gripla*, 25 (2016), pp. 93–125.

13. CRIMINAL PROFILING

Barraclough, Eleanor Rosamund, 'Inside Outlawry in Grettis saga Ásmundarsonar and Gísla saga Súrssonar: Landscape in the Outlaw Sagas', *Scandinavian Studies*, 82 (2010), pp. 365–88.

Bessason, Haraldur, and Robert J. Glendinning, eds, *Laws of Early Iceland: Grágás I, the Codex Regius of Grágás, with Material from Other Manuscripts*, vol. 3, trans. Andrew Dennis et al. (Winnipeg: University of Manitoba Press, 2006).

Brink, Stefan, 'Law and Society', in Stefan Brink and Neil Price, eds, *The Viking World* (London: Routledge, 2008), pp. 23–31.

Byock, Jesse, 'The Icelandic Althing: Dawn of Parliamentary Democracy', in J. M. Fladmark, ed., *Heritage and Identity: Shaping the Nations of the North* (Shaftsbury, Dorset: Donhead, 2002), pp. 1–18.

Díaz-Vera, Javier E., and Teodoro Manrique Antón, '"Better shamed before one than shamed before all": Shaping Shame in Old English and Old Norse texts', in Javier Díaz-Vera, ed., *Metaphor and Metonymy across Time and Cultures: Perspectives on the Sociohistorical Linguistics of Figurative Language* (Berlin: Mouton de Gruyter, 2015), pp. 225–64.

Faulkes, Anthony, ed., *A New Introduction to Old Norse, Part II: Reader* (4th edition) (Exeter: Viking Society for Northern Research, University College London, 2007), http://www.vsnrweb-publications.org.uk/NION-2a.pdf [accessed 14.09.18].

Jakobsson, Ármann, 'The Specter of Old Age: Nasty Old Men in the

Sagas of Icelanders', *Journal of English and Germanic Philology*, 104/3 (July 2005), pp. 297–325.

Miller, William Ian, *Humiliation and Other Essays on Honor, Social Discomfort, and Violence* (Ithaca, NY: Cornell University Press, 1993).

Phelpstead, Carl, 'Size Matters: Penile Problems in Sagas of Icelanders', *Exemplaria*, 19/3 (2007), pp. 420–37.

Porter, Edel, and Teodoro Manrique Antón, 'Flushing in Anger, Blushing in Shame: Somatic Markers in Old Norse Emotional Expressions', *Cognitive Linguistic Studies*, 2/1 (January 2015), pp. 24–49.

Redpath, I. D., 'Notes on the Text of the *Scriptores Physiognomonici*', *The Classical Quarterly*, 56/2 (December 2006), pp. 603–06.

Wills, Tarrin Jon, 'Testosterone, Aggression and Status in Early Northern Literature', *Northern Studies*, 44 (2013), pp. 60–79.

———, 'Physiology and Behaviour in the Sagas', *Viking and Medieval Scandinavia*, 8 (2012), pp. 279–97.

14. BIRDS

Baraz, Daniel, *Medieval Cruelty: Changing Perceptions, Late Antiquity to the Early Modern Period* (Ithaca, NY: Cornell University Press, 2003).

Bourns, Timothy, 'The Language of Birds in Old Norse Tradition' (MA thesis, University of Iceland, 2012).

Chadd, Rachel Warren, and Marianne Taylor, *Birds: Myth, Lore & Legend* (London: Bloomsbury, 2016).

Dobat, Andres Siegfried, 'Viking Stranger Kings: The Foreign as a Source of Power in Viking Age Scandinavia, or, Why There Was a Peacock in the Gokstad Ship Burial?', *Early Medieval Europe*, 23/2 (May 2015), pp. 161–201.

Dove, Carla J., and Stephen Wickler, 'Identification of Bird Species Used to Make a Viking Age Feather Pillow', *Arctic*, 69/1 (March 2016), pp. 29–36.

Edda Sæmundar hinns Fróða (*The Edda of Sæmund the Learned*), trans. Benjamin Thorpe (London: Trübner & Co, 1907).

Einarsson, Bjarni, '*De Normanorum Atrocitate*, or on the Execution of Royalty by the Aqueline Method', *Saga-Book of the Viking Society*, 22 (1988), pp. 79–82.

———, and Roberta Frank, 'The Blood-Eagle Once More: Two Notes', *Saga-Book of the Viking Society*, 23 (1990), pp. 80–83.

Frank, Roberta, 'The Blood-Eagle Again', *Saga-Book of the Viking Society*, 22 (1988), pp. 287–9.

——, 'Viking Atrocity and Skaldic Verse: The Rite of the Blood-Eagle', *English Historical Review*, 99/391 (1984), pp. 332–43.

Gotfredsen, A. B., 'Birds in Subsistence and Culture at Viking Age Sites in Denmark', *International Journal of Osteoarchaeology*, 24/3 (May/June 2014), pp. 365–77.

Hutton, Ronald, *The Pagan Religions of the Ancient British Isles: Their Nature and Legacy* (Oxford: Blackwell, 1991).

Lindow, John, *Norse Mythology: A Guide to the Gods, Heroes, Rituals, and Beliefs* (Oxford: Oxford University Press, 2001).

Orchard, Andy, *Dictionary of Norse Myth and Legend* (London: Cassell, 1997).

Pluskowski, Aleks, 'Apocalyptic Monsters: Animal Inspirations for the Iconography of Medieval Northern Devourers', in Bettina Bildhauer and Robert Mills, eds, *The Monstrous Middle Ages* (Toronto: University of Toronto Press, 2004), pp. 155–76.

The Poetic Edda, trans. Henry Adams Bellows (New York: Princeton University Press, 1936).

The Prose Edda, trans. Jesse Byock (London: Penguin, 2005).

Rollanson, David, 'Ælle [Ælla] (d. 867)', *Oxford Dictionary of National Biography* (Oxford: Oxford University Press, 2004).

Smyth, A. P., *Scandinavian Kings in the British Isles, 850–880* (Oxford: Oxford University Press, 1977).

15. LUCK

Andrén, Anders, 'Behind "Heathendom": Archaeological Studies of Old Norse Religion', *Scottish Archaeological Journal*, 27/2 (2005), pp. 105–138.

Bates, David and Robert Liddiard, eds, *East Anglia and Its North Sea World in the Middle Ages* (Woodbridge, Suffolk: Boydell & Brewer, 2013).

Blinkenberg, C. S., *The Thunderweapon in Religion and Folklore* (Cambridge: Cambridge University Press, 1911).

Carelli, P., 'Thunder and Lightning, Magical Miracles. On the Popular Myth of Thunderbolts and the Presence of Stone Age Artefacts in Medieval Deposits', in Hans Andersson, Peter Carelli and Lars Ersgård, eds, *Visions of the Past: Trends and Traditions in Swedish Medieval Archaeology* (Lund Studies in Medieval Archaeology, 9) (Stockholm: Riksantivarieämbetet & Institute of Archaeology, University of Lund, 1997), pp. 393–417.

Causey, Faya, *Amber and the Ancient World* (Los Angeles: Getty Publications, 2011).

Davidson, H. R. Ellis, 'Thor's Hammer', *Folklore*, 76/1 (1965), pp. 1–15.

Grönbech, Vilhelm, *The Culture of the Teutons*, trans. W. Worster (London: Oxford University Press, 1931).

Hallberg, Peter, 'The Concept of Gipta-gaefa-hamingja in Old Norse Literature', in Peter Foot et al., eds, *Proceedings of the First International Saga Conference* (London: Viking Society for Northern Research, 1973), pp. 141–74.

Hansen, Gitte, *Everyday Products in the Middle Ages: Crafts, Consumption and the Individual in Northern Europe c. AD 800–600* (Oxford: Oxbow Books, 2015).

Hurstwic, 'Honor, Dueling, and Drengskapr in the Viking Age', http://www.hurstwic.org/history/articles/society/text/drengur.htm [accessed 14.09.18].

Lal, Chandar, '(Re)visions of Royal Luck in the Sagas of Óláfr Tryggvason', *Viking and Medieval Scandinavia*, 10 (2014), pp. 99–128.

MacLeod, Mindy, and Bernard Mees, *Runic Amulets and Magic Objects* (Woodbridge, Suffolk: Boydell & Brewer, 2006).

Norwegian Institute for Cultural Heritage Research, 'Unusual Medieval Dice Found in Bergen', https://niku.no/en/2018/03/uvanlig-terning-middelalderen-funnet-bergen/ [accessed 14.09.18].

Sommer, Bettina Sejbjerg, 'The Norse Concept of Luck', *Scandinavian Studies*, 79/3 (2007), pp. 275–94.

Staecker, J., 'Thor's Hammer: Symbol of Christianization and Political Delusion', *Lund Archaeological Review*, 5 (1999), pp. 89–104.

Turville-Petre, E. O. G., *Myth and Religion of the North: The Religion of Ancient Scandinavia* (New York: Holt, Rinehart & Winston, 1964).

16. FRIENDSHIP

Arnold, Bettina, '"Drinking the Feast": Alcohol and the Legitimation of Power in Celtic Europe', *Cambridge Archaeological Journal*, 9/1 (April 1999), pp. 71–93.

de Vegvar, Carol Neuman, 'Dining with Distinction: Drinking Vessels and Difference in the Bayeux Tapestry Feast Scenes', in Michael J. Lewis, Gale R. Owen-Crocker and Dan Terkla, eds, *The Bayeux Tapestry: New Approaches* (Oxford: Oxbow Books, 2011), pp. 112–20.

Dietler, Michael, 'Feasting and Fasting', in Timothy Ingersoll, ed., *The Oxford Handbook on the Archaeology of Ritual and Religion* (Oxford: Oxford University Press, 2011), pp. 179–94.

Etting, Vivian, *The Story of the Drinking Horn: Drinking Culture in Scandinavia during the Middle Ages* (University Press of Southern Denmark, 2013).

Graham-Campbell, James, *The Viking World* (London: Frances Lincoln, 2013).

Karnell, Maria Herlin, ed., *Gotland's Picture Stones: Bearers of an Enigmatic Legacy* (Gotländskt Arkiv, 2012).

Lucas, Gavin, ed., *Hofstaðir: Excavations of a Viking Age Feasting Hall in North-Eastern Iceland* (Institute of Archaeology Monograph Series, 1) (Reykjavík: Fornleifastofnun Íslands, 2009).

MacGregor, Arthur, *Bone, Antler, Ivory & Horn: The Technology of Skeletal Materials since the Roman Period* (London: Taylor & Francis, 1985).

Oehrl, Sigmund, 'Documenting and Interpreting the Picture Stones of Gotland: Old Problems and New Approaches', *Current Swedish Archaeology*, 25 (2017), pp. 87–122.

Riseley, Charles Prescott, 'Ceremonial Drinking in the Viking Age' (unpublished MA thesis, University of Oslo, 2014).

Rood, Joshua, 'Drinking With Óðinn: Alcohol and Religion in Heathen Scandinavia' (unpublished MA dissertation, University of Iceland, 2014).

Sigurðsson, Jón Viðar, *Viking Friendship: The Social Bond in Iceland and Norway, c. 900–1300* (Ithaca, NY: Cornell University Press, 2017).

——, 'The Wedding at Flugumýri in 1253: Icelandic Feasts between the Free State Period and Norwegian Hegemony', in Wojtek Jezierski et al., eds, *Rituals, Performatives, and Political Order in Northern Europe, c. 650–1350* (Turnhout: Brepols, 2015), pp. 209–35.

Ward, Christie L., 'Norse Drinking Traditions' (paper presented at the Alexandrian Company Symposium on Food and Festival in the Middle Ages, 2001), http://www.vikinganswerlady.com/resume/worksamples/NorseDrinkingTraditions.pdf [accessed 14.09.18].

17. FUN

Caldwell, D. H., M. A. Hall and C. Wilkinson, 'The Lewis Hoard of Gaming Pieces: A Re-examination of their Context, Meanings, Discovery and Manufacture', *Medieval Archaeology*, 53/1 (November 2009), pp. 155–203.

Gardeła, Leszek, 'What the Vikings Did For Fun?: Sports and pastimes in Medieval Northern Europe', *World Archaeology*, 44/2 (2012), pp. 234–47.

Gogosz, R., 'Horse-fights: The Brutal Entertainment of the Icelanders in the Middle Ages', *Średniowiecze Polski i Powszechne*, 5/9 (2014), pp. 17–32.

Hall, Mark A., 'Board Games in Boat Burials: Play in the Performance of Migration and Viking Age Mortuary Practice', *European Journal of Archaeology*, 19/3 (2016), pp. 439–55.

Jochens, Jenny M., *Women in Old Norse Society* (Ithaca, NY: Cornell University Press, 1995).

Rundqvist, M., and H. Williams, 'A Viking Boat Grave with Amber Gaming Pieces Excavated at Skamby, Östergötland, Sweden', *Medieval Archaeology*, 52 (2008), pp. 69–102.

Short, William R., *Icelanders in the Viking Age: The People of the Sagas* (Jefferson, NC: McFarland & Company, 2010).

Thurber, B. A., 'The Viking Ball Game', *Scandinavian Studies*, 87/2 (Summer 2015), pp. 167–88.

Williams, Mary, *Social Scandinavia in the Viking Age* (New York: Macmillan, 1920).

18. DOUBLE STANDARDS

Frank, Roberta, 'Marriage in Twelfth- and Thirteenth-Century Iceland', *Viator*, 4 (1973), pp. 473–84.

Hedenstierna-Jonson, C., et al., 'A Female Viking Warrior Confirmed by Genomics', *American Journal of Physical Anthropology*, 164 (2017), pp. 853–60.

Jesch, Judith, 'Let's Debate Female Viking Warriors Yet Again', Norse and Viking Ramblings, http://norseandviking.blogspot.com/2017/09/lets-debate-female-viking-warriors-yet.html, 9 September 2017 [accessed 21.08.18].

——, 'Viking Women', BBC History, http://www.bbc.co.uk/history/ancient/vikings/women_01.shtml, 29 March 2011 [accessed 21.08.18].

——, *Women in the Viking Age* (Woodbridge: Boydell, 1991).

Jochens, Jenny M., *Women in Old Norse Society* (Ithaca, NY: Cornell University Press, 1995).

——, 'Consent in Marriage: Old Norse Law, Life and Literature', *Scandinavian Studies*, 58/2 (1986), pp. 142–76.

National Museum of Denmark, 'Women in the Viking Age', https://en.natmus.dk/historical-knowledge/denmark/prehistoric-period-until-1050-ad/the-viking-age/the-people/women/ [accessed 21.08.18]

O'Sullivan, Joanne, 'Strung Along: Re-evaluating Gendered Views of Viking-Age Beads', *Medieval Archaeology*, 59/1 (2015), pp. 73–86.

Thomas, Keith, 'The Double Standard', *Journal of the History of Ideas*, 20/2 (1959), pp. 195–216.

Wicker, Nancy L., 'Nimble-Fingered Maidens in Scandinavia: Women as Artists and Patrons', in Therese Martin, ed., *Reassessing the Roles of Women as 'Makers' of Medieval Art and Architecture* (Leiden: Brill, 2012), pp. 865–902.

19. SILK

Barisitz, Stephan, *Central Asia and the Silk Road: Economic Rise and Decline over Several Millennia* (Berlin: Springer, 2017).

Coatsworth, Elizabeth, and Gale Owen-Crocker, *Clothing the Past: Surviving Garments from Early Medieval to Early Modern Western Europe* (Leiden, Netherlands: Brill, 2018).

de La Vaissière, Étienne, *Sogdian Traders: A History* (Leiden, Netherlands: Brill, 2005).

Frankopan, Peter, *The Silk Roads: A New History of the World* (London: Bloomsbury, 2015).

Huang, Angela Ling, and Carsten Jahnke, eds, *Textiles and the Medieval Economy: Production, Trade, and Consumption of Textiles, 8th–16th Centuries* (Oxford: Oxbow Books, 2015).

Kennedy, Hugh, *The Great Arab Conquests: How the Spread of Islam Changed the World We Live In* (Philadelphia, PA: Da Capo Press, 2007).

20. STAFFS

Bill, Jan, 'Protecting Against the Dead?: On the Possible Use of Apotropaic Magic in the Oseberg Burial', *Cambridge Archaeological Journal*, 26/1 (2016), pp. 141–55.

Brunning, Sue, 'A "Divination Staff" from Viking-Age Norway at the British Museum', *Acta Archaeologica*, 87/1 (2016), pp. 193–200.

Gardeta, Leszek, 'Entangled Worlds: Archaeologies of Ambivalence in the Viking Age' (unpublished PhD thesis, University of Aberdeen, 2012).

———, 'A Biography of the Seiðr-Staffs: Towards an Archaeology of Emotions', in L. P. Słupecki and J. Morawiec, eds, *Between Paganism and Christianity in the North* (Rzeszów: Rzeszów University, 2009), pp. 190–219.

————, 'Into Viking Minds: Re-interpreting the Staffs of Sorcery and Unraveling Seiðr', *Viking and Medieval Scandinavia*, 4 (2008), pp. 45–84.

Jesch, Judith, *Women in the Viking Age* (Woodbridge, Suffolk: Boydell & Brewer, 1991).

National Museum of Denmark, 'The Magic Wands of Viking Seeresses?', https://en.natmus.dk/historical-knowledge/denmark/prehistoric-period-until-1050-ad/the-viking-age/religion-magic-death-and-rituals/the-magic-wands-of-the-seeresses/ [accessed 22.08.18].

Price, Neil, *The Viking Way: Magic and Mind in Late Iron Age Scandinavia / Religion and War in the Later Iron Age of Scandinavia* (Oxford: Oxbow Books, 2017).

———, 'Sorcery and Circumpolar Traditions in Old Norse Belief', in Stefan Brink and Neil Price, eds, *The Viking World* (London: Routledge, 2008), pp. 244–8.

———, 'The Archaeology of Seiðr: Circumpolar Traditions in Viking Pre-Christian Religion', in S. Lewis-Simpson, ed., *Vinland Revisited: The Norse World at the Turn of the First Millennium* (St. John's, NL: HSANL, 2004), pp. 277–94.

———, 'Viking Age Sorcerers', *Viking Heritage Magazine*, 4 (2004), pp. 21–4.

———, 'Viking Age Sorcery', *Viking Heritage Magazine*, 3 (2004), pp. 3–6.

ILLUSTRATION CREDITS

p. 1 Viking helm found in Gjermundbu, Norway, tenth century (*Mary Evans/Iberfoto*); p. 11 Viking Age key (*Lennart Larsen/National Museum, Denmark*); p. 17 Viking graffiti, Hagia Sophia, Istanbul (*Wikimedia Commons*); p. 19 Sketch of graffiti depicting Viking ship, Hagia Sophia, Istanbul (*Thomas Thomov, 'Four Scandinavian Ship Graffiti from Hagia Sophia', Byzantine and Modern Greek Studies, 38/2, 2014*); p. 25 Coin of Erik Bloodaxe (*Tine Bonde Christensen/National Museum, Denmark*); p. 31 Depiction of Loki, the Viking god of mischief, eighteenth century (*Wikimedia Commons*); p. 35 Sketch of the 'Snaptun Stone' (*oneofamyriadfaces. wordpress.com*); p. 39 Hair from a tenth-century cremation grave (*Swedish History Museum*); p. 45 Hot bath at Reykholt, Iceland (*Pavel Dobrovsky/Shutterstock*); p. 53 The ninth-century Oseberg Ship during its excavation (*Chronicle/Alamy Stock Photo*); p. 61 Viking-style Norman ships depicted in the Bayeux Tapestry, eleventh century (*DEA/M. SEEMULLER/Getty Images*); p. 77 Filed teeth from Viking remains (*Oxford Archaeology/Bnps/Shutterstock);* p. 83 Gotland image stone (*Wikimedia Commons*); p. 89 Illustration from Snorre Sturluson: *Heimskringla*, J.M. Stenersen & Co, 1899 (*Wikimedia Commons*); p. 95 Egill Skallagrímsson in a seventeenth-century manuscript of *Egil's saga* (*The Picture Art Collection/ Alamy Stock Photo*); p. 101 A coin of Anlaf Guthfrithsson (*Tine Bonde Christensen/National Museum, Denmark*); p. 109 A playing die, c.1400 (*SWNS*); p. 113 A Thor's Hammer made from amber (*vikingage.org*); p. 117 Drinking scene depicted on Gotland stone

(*PHAS/Getty Images*); p. 123 Silver-gilt drinking horn fittings found at Sutton Hoo (*Public domain*); p. 125 The Lewis Chessmen (*CM Dixon/Print Collector/Getty Images*); p. 133 Silver figure of woman, found at Tissø, Denmark (*Roberto Fortuna & Kira Ursem/National Museum, Denmark*); p. 141 Fragment of silk from the Oseberg ship burial (© *2019 Kulturhistorisk museum, UiO*); p. 147 Two iron divination staffs (*Arnold Mikkelsen/National Museum, Denmark*)

While every effort has been made to contact copyright-holders of illustrations, the authors and publisher would be grateful for information about any illustrations where they have been unable to trace them, and would be glad to make amendments in further editions.

INDEX